A Guide to Business Principles and Practices for Interior Designers

A Guide to Business Principles and Practices for Interior Designers

NEW REVISED EDITION

by Harry Siegel, C.P.A., with Alan Siegel, Esq.

WHITNEY LIBRARY OF DESIGN
an imprint of Watson-Guptill Publications/New York

DEDICATION
This book is dedicated to my wife, Elaine, for her contribution of encouragement and patience and for developing an orderly approach for presenting the material in this book; to Cheryl for her encouragement, patience, and sacrifice of time which enabled Alan to complete his contribution to this revised book; to Carol, Jerry, Jackie, Jon, Shari, and Jamie Beth for *believing*.

Copyright © 1982 by Harry Siegel and Alan M. Siegel

Chapter 24 © 1982 by Jerrold M. Sonet

First published in 1982 in New York by Whitney Library of Design, an imprint of Watson-Guptill Publications, a division of Billboard Publications, Inc., 1515 Broadway, New York, N.Y. 10036

Library of Congress Cataloging in Publication Data
Siegel, Harry.
  A guide to business principles and practices for interior designers.
  Includes index.
  1. Interior decoration—Practice. I. Siegel,
Alan M., 1948–   II. Title.
NK2116.S5   1982   747′.023′73   82-6981
ISBN 0-8230-7252-5   AACR2

16 17   18 19   20/04 03 02 01 00

**Forms illustrated in this book
can be obtained from:**

Interior Designers Forms Company
Division of Murphy/Simon Printing
Co., Inc.
1280 Saw Mill River Road
North Yonkers, NY 10710
(914) 968-7741

Send $2 for forms catalog
(credited to first purchase)

Edited by Susan Davis and Stephen A. Kliment
Designed by Jay Anning
Graphic production by Ellen Greene
Set in 11 point Century Schoolbook

Contents

ACKNOWLEDGMENTS

The authors feel that they—and all designers and students who may find this book useful—owe a debt of gratitude to the interior designers and associates who encouraged them to write it and who provided so many of the experiences and case histories that pointed out the need for the first edition and this revised edition. Thanks for essential inspiration and help are due to the many designers who cooperated by giving permission to reproduce many of the paper office forms that were developed for their practices.

The authors take this opportunity to acknowledge our gratitude and thanks to:

Everett Brown, FASID, who first suggested the need for the book and who encouraged Harry Siegel to proceed with the formidable task of writing it.

Rita St. Clair, FASID (past president of the American Society of Interior Designers), who is committed to "professionalism in interior design" and who gave Harry the opportunity and encouragement to write the first manual, "Fees and Compensations" (1967), for the AID, which launched subsequent books on business practices.

Jerrold M. Sonet, senior partner of the New York law firm, Levy & Sonet, who contributed Chapter 24, The Interior Designer as a Product Designer. His friendship, expertise, cooperation, and input were invaluable in developing the rationale for many of the business practices outlined in the book.

Henry F. Schoenfeld, president of Schoenfeld Insurance Associates, Inc. (Baltimore, Md.), exclusive agency for Interior Designers Professional Liability Insurance, for his authoritative advice and Chapter 27, Insurance.

Albert Siegel, CPA, and Steven Sacks, CPA, Harry's former partners, whose practical experiences added so much to the dimensions of the material included in the book.

American Society of Interior Designers (and its forerunners AID and NSID) for the insights into the profession that we derived from our association with them and for affording us, along with the other professional organizations, seminar platforms for discussions on the subject of business practices and procedures.

Stephen A. Kliment, FAIA, Senior Editor of the Whitney Library of Design, who deserves special thanks for suggesting the need to revise and update the book, who spent many hours with the authors reviewing the material, and who suggested and guided the approach to the arduous task of rewriting and updating and kept after us until it was completed.

Susan Davis, Development Editor of the Whitney Library of Design, for her enthusiasm, suggestions, and editorial expertise that made it possible to see this work completed.

Prologue

It gives me great pleasure to introduce this book to interior design students, to those interior designers entering the field, and to my colleagues. Many of you are already familiar with the original of this revised and updated version of Harry Siegel's work. It has served the profession as the most complete and definitive book on the subject of business practices and procedures for use in the designer's office. The original book not only has been used as a text in the educational system, but is also found on the reference shelf of most interior design studios and offices in allied professional fields.

To fully understand and appreciate the present revised work, it is important, as well as interesting, to look back to the profession as it was when the original book was published in 1968 and to become aware of the increased sophistication of skills that the interior designer needs to perform today. The 50s and 60s were important years for the profession as the title of *interior designer* first came into general use to describe the work of a new professional. This practitioner emerged to offer a new and different kind of expertise, based largely on a combination of knowledge from such areas as the decorative arts, interior decorating, and architecture. This new term was also popularized by the professional design associations and the press that identified and illustrated the tasks and finished work of the interior designer and that were greatly responsible for creating consumer awareness and the resulting acceptance.

Interior design, as it was practiced then, is an American phenomenon, and many still consider it an American invention. It evolved and blossomed in a climate most sympathetic to its development—favorable economic times, aggressive professional organizations, and a receptive, affluent consumer public.

It was an exciting time for many of us who were just starting our practices. We were, compared with today's profession, few in number. Most of us were well trained to conceptualize and detail our designs for the client. But we also recognized the absence of standards and consequent lack of professional posture that we communicated to the client in such areas as letters of agreement, methods of billing, purchasing, and general organization of the work. It became apparent that guidelines had to be developed not only in areas of office business procedures, but also in methods of computing fees and markups on the purchase of merchandise. My interest in seeing such guidelines resulted in the formation of a business procedures committee under the auspices of what was then the American Institute of Interior Designers (AID) that I chaired in 1965.

At the beginning of the research it became obvious that each design office had its own methods of operation. Many were based on general business and accounting procedures that, even though acceptable in principle, did not meet the special needs of our work. Others often invented their own methods and barely managed to survive because of what is often considered the malaise of the profession—the designer's lack of organization and business sense.

But after all the data were in, a few studios did stand out as models of efficiency that resulted in successful and profitable practices. One of the common denominators that linked these firms was not only their design creativity but the creativity and understanding of our profession by business managers or advisors. Fortunately, in our profession, "Macy's does tell Gimbels," and Harry Siegel was often mentioned by a number of these stellar firms as their guru.

Since there seemed to be interest in the profession for more information on how to compute fees and for data on the various methods of compensation, Harry Siegel was asked to write a brochure for AID that would address these two issues. It certainly proved to be one of AID's most successful organizational efforts. The brochure then triggered a series of workshops throughout the country with Harry Siegel as featured speaker. The topics not only were the ones covered by the brochure, but dealt with all aspects of business practice for the designer.

The overwhelming response to the brochure and the workshops clearly showed the need for a more complete publication that would not only serve the AID's members, but the entire profession. As a response to this need, the first edition of *A Guide to Business Principles and Practices for Interior Designers* was written and published by the Whitney Library of Design in 1968.

Today's designer is not only a conceptualist, but a space planner, a project manager, a designer of products, at all times operating with ease in both residential and nonresidential spaces. In the realm of corporate offices and such public spaces as hotels and restaurants, hardly a project is started without the interior designer as one of the design team. It is no wonder that this comparatively new profession has now attained international status and is accepted as a legitimate occupation throughout the world.

The expanded scope of services now offered by the design office has also increased the body of knowledge and the responsibilities that the designer must be able to meet. I am sure you will agree after reading this revised edition of *A Guide to Business Principles and Practices for Interior Designers* that you will be able to meet these new challenges and work within the changing demands that affect our work. The book is successful because it remains based on the same sound principles and practices, but it now reflects the broader responsibilities that our profession has taken on by necessity as well as choice.

Rita St. Clair, FASID
President
Rita St. Clair Associates, Inc.

About the Indispensable Role of Business Practice in the Highly Artistic Profession of Interior Design

The purpose of this book is to make the professional interior designer aware of basic business principles that he or she must heed to practice the profession with reasonable monetary rewards, with the confidence of the community, and without wasting energy or resources on business problems. In addition the book describes procedures and forms that are mandatory. It does not enter the area of the interior designer's professional qualifications such as artistic skills, creativity, or knowledge, though in analyzing business principles it refers to them.

This book is intended for interior designers in many different stages of their careers and in many different branches of the profession:

For the practicing interior designer—to show him or her how to analyze and solve operational problems, as well as to provide a multitude of essential paper forms, such as clients' inventory forms, billing controls, trade source forms, and budget estimate forms—which enable interior design firms to systematize and control the flow of operations, money, materials, and commitments.

For professional interior designers employed in interior design firms or in the interior design departments of other types of firms—to give them necessary insight into operations that they may not find easy to observe clearly or wholly on the job.

For architects who maintain interior design departments in their firms in order to complete the interiors of their own buildings—as well as *for architects who specialize or hope to specialize in interior design*—to give them a clear picture of the logistics of interior design operations.

For the managers of shops, wholesale establishments, and contract firms that employ professional interior designers in order to provide their customers with design service—so that they also may grasp the logistics of interior design.

For the officers of corporations and institutions that maintain their own salaried staffs of interior designers to produce the interiors of their own premises—as well as *for the officers of such corporations and institutions who have occasion to engage independent interior design firms* for this work—to answer their questions on sound conduct in the field.

For the neophyte who hopes to go into practice—to outline the steps which he or she must take to set up an office or to associate with one—and to describe the different forms that the firm can take, depending on the designer's needs and inclinations.

For the student—to confront him or her with the reality that a career in interior design means a career in business as well as in the highly esthetic art which dominates his or her attention during the years of professional training.

Interior design is an art. And—like all professions—it can be defined simultaneously as a profession *and* as a business. The definition and branches of the profession of interior design are covered briefly in Chapter 1, but here, in stating the purpose of this book, it is pertinent to stress the unusual importance of sound business practice in this profession. *All* professions involve business transactions, but they vary markedly in the complexity of these transactions: physicians, dentists, and lawyers pay rent, hire assistants, keep records, and send bills. But interior designers, architects, and engineers must carry through financial transactions on a very different level of complexity—and among the professions that are complex from the standpoint of business, interior design is the most misunderstood.

Partly the misunderstanding is the result of the fact that interior design has not been recognized and clearly defined as a profession for a period comparable to many of the others. Partly the misunderstanding is the direct outcome of an apparent paradox inherent in the financial transactions of the field. Often, instead of being paid like a professional person for his or her services, the interior designer appears to be paid like a merchant for the considerable value of material goods purchased for the interior, and it is not easy to explain that it is actually his or her skill in choosing and composing and handling the goods for which he or she is being paid. The confusion is only compounded by transactions whereby the interior designer is paid both for goods and for services—and on the basis, moreover, of systems of accounting that to the outside observer appear to be mysterious and inconsistent.

But interior design *is* complex—as an art, as a profession, *and* as a business. There is nothing wrong with that. People are complex, their lives are complex, our economy is complex, spaces are complex. What *is* wrong is that many interior designers who practice their *art* and their *profession* with undeniable competence—even with brilliant resourcefuless—fail to make a go of their careers because they do not know how to cope with their *business*. Without sound business practice, interior design is a minefield loaded with explosive charges of financial disasters, tarnished reputations, catastrophic client relations, sleepless nights.

Unfortunately few candidates for the profession are aware of these hazards. yet the business principles that must be borne in mind to practice interior design with reasonable financial security can be grasped by any adult of competent mind. Mathematical genius is not required. With knowledge, counsel, and awareness, the designer should be able to cope with the business side of practice—without becoming obsessed or swamped by it. The first rule is to avoid venturing into the unknown territory of business without a guide. Early in his or her career the designer should obtain qualified business counsel.

The business fiascos that attend the careers of too many interior designers arise less from their inability to understand business principles than from their unwillingness to think seriously about business at all. They think of themselves as artists. It is fascination with line and form and color that propels them into the field as students. They are sensitive to space and proportion, mood and light. They enjoy the feel of materials—rich, rough, luscious, or fragile. They are excited by pattern. They see interiors as an expression of their clients' personalities, as solutions for psychological needs and functional requirements. They want to make people comfortable and to make difficult spaces work.

They look forward to the creation of settings that will instill flavor and drama in living—like decor for plays onstage. They love to track down *objets de vertu* and to exploit works of art as magnets for the eye and cues to the imagination.

Office procedures, multiple forms, contracts, percentages? What do they care about such things?

This book brings to the attention of both the new and the practicing interior designer the business procedures of this field, so that they will have an awareness of sound and proper business conduct under the conditions that will face them in the course of professional practice. The authors have spent many years working with interior designers, solving their business problems, and developing forms and systems to reduce burdensome chores into efficient routines and clarify the control of operations. In this book they have avoided the technical jargon of accounting, finance, and legal problems, but have—in simple, direct language—presented a picture of the business operations of an interior design office from its formation through all ramifications of its dealings with clients and trade sources. In each stage they have pinpointed the problems typical of that phase and outlined guides to cope with them.

Olga Gueft

PART 1

A Practice in Interior Design and How to Establish One

Interior Design as a Profession

Profession:

> a vocation or occupation requiring advanced training in some liberal art or science, and usually involving mental rather than manual work
>
> *Webster's New World Dictionary*

What we mean by the word *profession* was clearly understood by the general public long before the dictionary writers made it official. The term *interior designer*, however, was hardly in use at all until about five decades ago and did not formally supersede the word *decorator* until the midfifties. At that time the two leading American organizations representing the profession made it part of their names. The elder, founded in 1931, acknowledged the obsolescence of *decorator* in 1961 when it changed its name from the American Institute of Decorators to the American Institute of Interior Designers (without changing its insignia initials, AID). The younger organization used the term from the outset, calling itself the National Society of Interior Designers (NSID) since its founding in 1957. On January 1, 1975, the American Society of Interior Designers (ASID) was formed through the consolidation of these two organizations, and it is now the largest organization representing professional interior designers. Another emerging organization is The Institute of Business Designers (IBD), dedicated solely to the professional designer whose major field is commercial and institutional interiors.

The history of the profession is beyond the scope of this book, but a brief survey will show why the change in terminology is significant. Throughout the recorded past, interiors have been designed and furnished by people operating under innumerable vocational guises and with as many different relationships to the patron or client on the one hand and to the workers, artisans, and suppliers on the other. Interiors have been produced by architects, builders, artists, sculptors, artist-craftsmen, artisans, upholsterers, drapers, cabinetmakers, shopkeepers, antique dealers, and, after World

War I, by imaginative, magnetic amateurs high on the social scale. It was with the advent of the very last group that the term *decorator* became important and popular.

People who understand that it is a misleading term still prefer to use it in conversation today, because the term *interior designer* is, to be sure, a rather more awkward mouthful. But *decorator* is ambiguous; it can mean a painter or paperhanger; it can mean a housewife with spare time on her hands and all the brass but none of the talent of the late Elsie de Wolfe, Lady Mendl—the original and greatest of the society decorators. *Interior designer* means a professional, and the ASID has defined his or her functions and qualifications very clearly:

> A professional interior designer is one who is qualified by education and experience to identify, research and creatively solve problems relative to the function and quality of man's proximate environment.
>
> His competency includes fundamental design, design analysis, space planning and programming, the design of all interior spaces and an understanding of other and related aspects of environmental design.
>
> He is recognized professionally after having completed accredited education and/or a minimum requirement in practical interior design or a related field.

The ASID along with other design organizations requires its candidates to pass a basic professional competency examination that is independently prepared and administered by the National Council for Interior Design Qualification (NCIDQ). In addition to professional qualifications, professional standards and ethics are demanded of practitioners:

> Members of the American Society of Interior Designers are required to conduct their professional practice in a manner that will command the respect and confidence of clients, suppliers, fellow professional designers and

the general public.
Excerpt from The Code of Ethics of the American Society of Interior Designers

Since the popular recognition of the phenomenon known as the *decorator* and the official definition of the professional *interior designer*, the profession has emerged as a distinct power on the American scene. Both in an economic and in an esthetic sense, the interior design profession is exerting an important, observable, and measurable influence on the American style of life. In capturing the imagination of the public, it has added as much to our awareness of the surroundings in our daily lives as to our intelligent handling of the factors of comfort, convenience, efficiency, and ease in the arrangement of the places where we live and work. It has added to our enjoyment of the sensuous and artistic components in our environment, as well as to our discrimination in appraising old and new objects of art and craftsmanship.

The emergence of the profession entails more, however, than capturing the imagination of the public. The national pocketbook is related as well, and we can go further and say that our commercial system is involved. The profession has developed in tandem with a distinct industry—the interior furnishings industry (a more accurate term than *home* furnishings industry). The operations of the interior furnishings industry reflect the enormous demand for quality products generated by the profession. It also makes possible the efficiency with which the profession can now provide what might be called custom or personal service on a mass scale. Working with "the trades," as they are known, which offer an amazing selection of products and services, the profession controls a sizable and steadily growing percentage of the discretionary expenditures of the public—both the individual and the corporate and institutional (including the government).

By the very definition of the word, interior designers are professionals. By the very impact of their work on society, they are professionals. By and large they conduct themselves as professionals in the esthetic and technical phases of their work. But when it comes to the business and financial aspects, too many still operate as rank amateurs. This can be disastrous, because budgeting and control of money for the desired esthetic result are as important a part of their service as the esthetic result. The very nature of the designer's service makes the financial aspect of the work complex, difficult—and essential. The designer does not usually stop at giving advice or producing drawings for interiors, but goes on to assume the responsibility for translating those ideas and drawings into tangible reality: specifying, ordering, and installing a huge dollar volume of goods and services. Herein lies the crucial importance of professionalism in the business aspects of interior design. It is not enough for the interior designer to achieve a professional level of competence in designing beautiful, appropriate, and functional interiors. It is also essential that he or she manage to achieve a professional level of competence in organizing his or her operation—whatever its size—in business dealings with clients, in business dealings with trade sources, in determining and collecting fees and other compensations, and in running his or her firm both on a short- and on a long-term basis. A profession with such economic impact needs to conduct its affairs in a rational manner, both to ensure a reasonable financial return to its members and to maintain its place in the economy.

Just where does the profession stand in the economy? Analysis of twelve design companies that were clients of my accounting firm is revealing. These firms range in size from the largest—with a staff of twelve designers doing a volume of over $1 million a year in gross billings—to the smallest—with one professional doing $100,000 in gross volume. In one year these twelve firms billed a total of $7,794,469 for goods, services, and fees and purchased for their clients $5,341,340 worth of goods and services. A recent national survey of 100 of the major nonresidential design firms indicated that they provided over $3 billion of interior furnishings, interior construction, and related services to their clients. If we assume that there are at least 15,000 design firms of unequivocally professional status in our country, it is safe to state that the interior design profession in the United States controls the flow of merchandise and services in the interior furnishings industry to an amount well in excess of $9 billion.

In summary, it is mandatory to view the profession as a major part of America's business scene and conduct ourselves in the sound, businesslike manner befitting the formal definition of a professional, and not as some wit has defined the interior designer: "Someone who tells you what kind of furniture to buy, what kind of draperies to hang, what colors to use around your house—sort of like a mother-in-law with a license."

Divisions of the Profession

The interior designer's function—to plan, design, and execute interiors of all kinds—encompasses a wide variety of services, a wide variety of business organizations offering such services, a wide variety of collaborative arrangements. Specialization is not compulsory in the profession, and there are many versatile designers or design firms that do many kinds of work; other designers may specialize in different kinds of work over a period of years. But the tendency to specialize is natural, and business conduct as well as professional activity follows well-established lines in each division of the profession.

The most important division is between residential and nonresidential interior design. Though many designers do both, it is nevertheless true that specialization in one or the other implies important differences in temperament, working habits, and business conduct.

RESIDENTIAL DESIGN

Residential interior design is for the *private* living quarters of *individuals* or individual families. We italicize the words *private* and *individuals* because the term *residential* is misleading. Hotels, school dormitories, and many kinds of institutions can be defined as residential, but are not included under the classification of residential interior design because the client is not the ultimate occupant, but a commercial or institutional entrepreneur who is preparing interiors for others to occupy. The relationship between client and designer is therefore different and less personal. In residential work much more time is usually spent by the designer in solving particular, one-of-a-kind details, and this has a decisive bearing on the economic or financial aspect of the work.

Residential interior design may encompass a whole residence or only a part of one. It may entail all the functions involved in creating the specific area, or only one or some. The job may include:

1. Planning, designing, executing, and furnishing

   a. A complete private house or apartment
   b. Only specified rooms or parts of rooms
2. Consultation or technical service on
   a. Color coordination
   b. Painting and wall covering schedules
   c. Specifications for specially built units
   d. Consultation with craftsmen or architects
   e. Developing layouts or floor plans
   f. Producing renderings, other presentations, working drawings

The personal nature of the client-designer relationship in residential work accounts for the fact that there are few hard-and-fast rules about exactly which services a designer may perform for a client. But there are certain clearly recognized tendencies, and it is therefore possible to generalize about what it takes to be a designer who is happy and successful when specializing in residential work. One may find interior designers in residential work who produce plans, room designs, and detail specifications for a fee and stop at that point, leaving the client to do his or her own purchasing. But this is the *exception* to the rule. The rule is that designers in the residential field do less drawing and detailing and more purchasing of single items than designers in the nonresidential field.

Under most conditions residential work does not pose insurmountable obstacles for the reasonably competent, reasonably businesslike interior designer. By reasonably competent we mean equipped with the talent and training required to design attractive and functional interiors. By reasonably businesslike we mean able to solve not only the design problems that are posed on the drawing board, but the practical problems of dealing with clients and workers and of finding one's way through the financial mazes of budgeting, billing, and collecting of that very essential commodity called money.

Paramount among the qualifications for personal satisfaction and success in the residential field are an interest in people and an ability to deal with them. This does not imply that the personal equation is not important in nonresidential work, but that it is more important in residential work. To put it bluntly, for each dollar earned, more hangs on the designer's insight and tact. The designer must in each case develop rapport with the client both culturally and financially. He must put his finger on the client's real needs, on his way of living and what it requires in functional facilities and esthetic background—whether or not the client can express it adequately or is even aware of just what it is. From the standpoint of working habits the designer must have sufficient patience and attention to detail to enable him to adhere meticulously to the realities of the client's budget. And as far as his professional equipment is concerned, thorough familiarity with market sources is primary—familiarity with line *and* prices (at least in general)—because residential work involves so many relatively small purchases of single items or small quantities that inefficiency in researching the market and shopping can create costly errors in completing design concepts.

If each residential job is to be a success from the client's point of view and profitable from the designer's, as well as enhance his or her reputation, following a sequence of working procedures is essential.

1. Careful interviewing to establish the client's program and budget.

2. Developing a design concept.

3. Obtaining client's approval of that concept.

4. Making estimates.

5. Making authorized purchases.

6. Supervising and installing.

A designer cannot rely completely on his or her esthetic performance. Success also depends on a firm understanding of the procedures needed to translate the concept into an interior well done and satisfactory financially as well as emotionally.

The designer must also be forearmed with a realistic awareness of his own shortcomings or gaps in his technical know-how. If any job calls for more than his grasp of electrical planning, air-conditioning, or architectural structure, he had better rely upon qualified architects, engineers, general contractors, and so on. And he had better know how to collaborate with them. It is sound practice to establish steady working relationships with experts and technicians who are likely to be needed on a long-term basis in the course of a career. It is impossible to be all things to all people; an attempt to do so can only lead to disaster.

NONRESIDENTIAL DESIGN

Nonresidential work includes all areas of concern to the business world, institutions, and government—hotels, motels, offices, banks, retail establishments large and small, schools, hospitals, other custodial institutions, showrooms, factories, museums, galleries, theaters, movies, restaurants, beauty parlors, gymnasiums, night clubs, discotheques, bowling alleys, and so on. In the field nonresidential work is sometimes loosely called *contract* work, implying a more formalized and precise business relationship between client and designer, as well as a different purchasing procedure for the characteristically larger quantities of goods and services involved.

Nonresidential work is becoming more important every year because the business community has come to accept the crucial importance of good professional interior design in determining the success of commercial enterprises. The client is not, as in residential work, the only person to be satisfied. The designer has also to consider the client's client—customers, employees, and the public in general. Success and failure are measured in the comings and goings of masses of people over a period of time; in the efficient or inefficient use of costly space; in efficient or inefficient circulation patterns that in turn affect the use of costly employee-hours. In addition the ability of employers to attract and hold competent employees essential to their operations and the replacement cycle of furnishings are other important criteria in judging a designer's work.

The client in nonresidential work is a businessperson or businesspersons—the corporate client or the board of trustees of an institution. The corporate client expects sound business thinking and methods from the interior designer. While a sound business approach ought to characterize residential work as well, it is an absolute must in nonresidental work.

Even to get the commission in nonresidential work, the designer must project the image of a responsible business organization. The selling approach must be highly organized long before the design concept is formulated. Either the client or the client's management consultant, or the architect or the interior designer must analyze the logistics of the client's operation in the premises to be designed; space planning may be a necessary prelude to the development of a design concept. (This is not to imply that a firm should invest time in planning research unless the client agrees to compensate for research time, whether or not the design firm gets the commission—a stricture that applies to all major time investments made in hopes of winning a commission. Chapter 20, Initial Client Contact in Nonresidential Work, covers this point more fully.)

The design firm in nonresidential work must be organized to proceed in logical steps somewhat more elaborate than in the residential field. After preparing rough layouts, the designer must translate that information into architectural drawings, construction specifications, electrical and ventilation requirements, working drawings, specifications for suppliers of materials and finally coordinate the work of the various trades and the installation.

To accomplish all this and deal rationally with clients, sources, and workers, the designer must have a well-organized office capable of solving design problems, expediting technical coordination, and carrying the load of paperwork needed to control each step of the operation. Last but not least, the designer must be sophisticated in balancing the financial factors of fees and costs that determine the profits of the operation.

INTERIOR DESIGN SERVICE IN RETAIL ESTABLISHMENTS

Many interior designers operate retail shops in which the retail operation may equal or surpass design service as a source of income. Often but not always, the owner-designer provides design service without charge while selling merchandise at retail, receiving compensation in the form of the normal profit. This type of enterprise calls for fairly ample capital to establish the business and maintain working inventory. The two phases of the operation tend to complement each other. The availability of attractively displayed merchandise attracts customers, and the availability of competent design services solves any problems that might arise, such as mistakes expensive to customers or—if the shop makes an exchange in such a case—to the shop. The rapid growth of interior design departments in large department and home furnishings stores testifies to the effectiveness of this kind of operation. So does the proliferation of office furniture dealerships that offer service in office design and space planning.

PRODUCT DESIGN BY INTERIOR DESIGNERS

Since the 1960s, we have witnessed the exciting expansion of interior designers into the product design field. A stroll through many of the nation's leading department stores will reveal the extent of this phenomena. Yet, in retrospect it is not a phenomena at all, but rather a natural extention of a designer's talent, education, and experience. The scholastic route to a diploma in interior design overlaps the scholastic route to a diploma in related design fields—including industrial and graphic design as well as the fine arts. Most interior design students are taught how to design fabrics and construct furniture.

Many interior designers actually design custom furniture, fabrics, and accessories for particular installations.

In view of this developing and challenging industry, a new chapter has been added to this book, Chapter 24, The Interior Designer as a Product Designer. Its purpose is to familiarize designers with the often difficult issues that a designer confronts attempting to enter into and operate in the field of product design.

ASSOCIATION IN ARCHITECTURAL, ENGINEERING, AND OTHER FIRMS

The new awareness of the importance of professionally designed interiors has had a noticeable effect on the practice of architecture. Many architects are eager to contract for the interiors of the buildings they design if these are owner-occupied. Many of the most prestigious architectural firms that had small or no interior departments ten or twenty years ago have large ones today. Of these a few even have a degree of autonomy, taking on interior commissions in collaboration with architectural firms other than their own.

A recent independent survey of the largest design firms in the country indicated that "approximately one-third of the top 100 are architectural firms with interior design departments." Architects have learned that there is a growing business in interior design, and they are making a tremendous impact on the field by the number of assignments they are obtaining.

The question of who gets the interior design job is decided by competitive bidding on the basis of both costs and concept. Obviously, the interior design firm that wants to swim along with this school of well-fed fish has to be completely in command of its procedures and vocabulary. In fact, it is not at all unusual to find architects employed in interior design firms of this class. To hold his or her own among them the interior designer must take systematic steps to learn how to:

1. Work in cooperation with architects.

2. Bid successfully in competition with architects.

3. Enhance the unique value of the interior designer's contribution on projects in which the various environmental professions work as a team.

Business Formations

No designer can set up a practice without first setting up a business organization. It shouldn't be necessary to make such a ridiculously obvious statement, but it is. Many designers commit themselves to the dream of making beautiful interiors happen without stopping to make the decisions and to go through the formalities that must be attended to before they have the legal right to do business. These decisions and formalities cannot be evaded even if the designer wants to start small—as small as a one-person office. For not even the one-person office can function until a business vehicle has been provided to roll it along. Such a vehicle can take one of four basic forms—the four business formations that are the subject of this chapter. They are defined and discussed in detail, after a brief introduction to the subject. The categories are

A. The individual form company

B. The associate relationship

C. The partnership

D. The corporation

Determining which one will best serve the needs and inclinations of the particular designer is the first step in launching a practice. It is also one of the most important decisions the designer will have to make, for each of these four forms has its own particular advantages and disadvantages relating to financing and operation. Far from being arbitrary, the choice should be calculated as rationally as possible. The design field in which the designer expects to practice—residential, nonresidential, product design, or all three—should be a critical factor. In addition there are fiscal and legal technicalities that make it advisable to get expert counsel from a Certified Public Accountant or lawyer experienced in the interiors field.

Before defining each of the four formations and discussing its advantages and disadvantages for interior designers, we want to point out that choosing one, though important, is not necessarily final and forever. A designer's practice may grow, change character, and develop new dimensions; the climate of business in which he or she operates may also change. Whatever decision a beginner makes, the experienced designer should periodically review it. It may be wise to consider a change if a practice has altered over the years.

The interior designer's decision on the form of business is more crucial than that of the architect or members of other professions because the interior designer has a far broader choice—one that is virtually unlimited. Most states now permit lawyers, physicians, accountants, and certain other professionals to incorporate. These are known as "professional corporations." But none of the other professionals is free—as the interior designer still is at present—to set themselves up in practice without first passing examinations and meeting other requirements for licenses. Unrestricted, the interior designer can choose any business structure he or she pleases, asking only, "What is best for me?"

A. INDIVIDUAL FORM

The simplest and least expensive business formation to organize is the *individual form,* also known as "sole proprietorship." In this form, the company and the individual owner are one and the same entity, so that the firm has no existence apart from the owner (and cannot continue after his or her death unless steps are taken to change it into one of the other types described in this chapter). In the individual form, the owner is both the controlling manager and the owner of all the company's assets. He or she receives all the profits and is personally responsible for all the losses.

To organize, the individual form does not require substantial legal formalities. All that is required is the following:

1. Deciding the location of the firm and its commercial style, that is, whether it will be an office, shop, home studio, or whatever.

2. Registering with such tax offices as is legally required. For example, sales taxes are levied in

most but not all states and in some but not all cities. Since the firm is expected to collect such taxes from its customers and give that money to the appropriate government office, the company must be registered with that government office and be issued an identifying "resale number." (Sales tax and its implications for interior designers is discussed in more detail in Chapter 18.)

3. Opening a bank account in the name of the firm.

4. Establishing credit and trade source relations.

5. Buying the necessary stationery and printed office forms (these forms are shown in various subsequent chapters).

However, before deciding to organize a company in the individual form, the designer should consider the following points:

1. Unlimited liability and its potential dangers.

2. Possible income tax disadvantages.

3. The question of the company name.

Each consideration will be discussed in detail.

1. UNLIMITED LIABILITY AND ITS POTENTIAL DANGERS

The individual form of business does not limit liabilities to the assets of the business. The owner is personally liable not only for all losses and debts but for every adverse effect of the operation. If the operation should become heavily in debt, creditors might proceed against the designer's personal assets that are not part of the regular business structure. It cannot be overemphasized that the individual form affords no protection in limiting liabilities, except those that may properly be covered by insurance. (Such liabilities are discussed in Chapter 27.)

The extent and nature of unlimited liability that may result from the operation of an individual form business should be reviewed by the designer's attorney, since these liabilities vary

in different parts of the country.

2. POSSIBLE INCOME TAX DISADVANTAGES

Since tax dollars are not minor in today's scheme of things, it is wise to examine the tax implications of this business formation. The designer will have to report the net income (or loss) of his business on his individual income tax return, listing the figures under Schedule C and adding them to his other income to arrive at his net taxable income. Since income tax rates rise on an escalating basis, the more the taxpayer reports as net taxable income, the higher the tax rate he will pay. This is of particular importance to those who have additional sources of income in the form of salaries, royalties, dividends, interest, capital gains, and so on. It is also significant to married designers whose spouses have their own incomes. In some cases the tax advantages that the couple might have gained by paying income taxes on a joint return may be counterbalanced by the high tax rate to be paid on the total income they report. The designer should have the tax consequences analyzed in light of his or her personal situation, comparing the taxes to be paid as an individual form of business with those to be paid as a corporate structure.

3. THE QUESTION OF THE COMPANY NAME

The new designer should be alert to the impression made by the name of his or her firm on trade sources and potential clients. The name should imply that the designer is a well-organized business entity. The firm's name is frequently the first tangible thing with which the designer makes contact with the business world. It should make a strong impression and help the designer build an image of stability and operational know-how. The name of an individual, which is the most likely and natural name for an individual form company, can imply a lack of organizational power and financial stability, with a dampening effect on credit applications in the trade, as well as on potential clients, particularly corporate clients. The "Inc.," "Ltd.," or "Corp." that can only be added to the name of an incorporated firm enhances its status immeasurably. This is not to imply that the owner's name is the only possible name for an individual form company. Designers often title their firms with assumed names—"Bon Mot Design Company"—or use their own names as the basis for an enlarged title—"Mary Jones Interiors Company." However, the designer who wishes to solve the name question with an assumed name must be aware that each community has its own legal requirements regarding their use. It is important to check this requirement in each community and to register the assumed name with the proper authorities.

B. ASSOCIATE STATUS

Before a designer decides to organize a company of his or her own, it may be worthwhile to consider an alternate working arrangement—to associate with an already organized company. Associate status is distinctly different from the position of an employee. Associate status offers many of the advantages of owning one's own business with very few of the disadvantages. It requires virtually no capital and risks none, but it allows the designer-associate as much freedom as the designer-owner to follow his or her own esthetic bent and to reap financial rewards—and full credit as well—for his or her own initiative, efficiency, and talent. The associate arrangement is excellent for both new and experienced designers. It gives the new designer the guidance and all the facilities of a going concern. It gives the experienced one a base from which to operate without being involved in the humdrum administrative chores and details of running an office.

What it *does* require is that the designer have something to offer to the company—perhaps "a following," that is, potential clients—or else an obvious and perhaps unusual talent or high degree of expertise in some phase of interior design in which the other associates of the firm

are relatively weak.

If the owner or owners of the firm invite a designer to join, the designer arranges to bring his or her work to the company, though making no investment and paying no concern to the administrative, financial, or personnel problems of the company. His or her responsibilities encompass client contact, all phases of planning and design, market research, the preparation of purchasing specifications, and supervision of the final installation. The company provides staff to perform all clerical work, actual ordering, payments to trade sources, and billing to clients.

Under this arrangement the designer and the company might share a fixed percentage of the gross profits of each job—the gross profit being the difference between the billing price to the client and the actual prime cost of tangible items and services provided. The designer's percentage may vary from perhaps 60 to 40 percent depending on the extent of the services rendered by the company. All normal operating and administrative expenses are paid for by the company and are not charged to the associate. The only exceptions are travel expenses, drafting, blueprints, and other cost items specific to each particular job.

In some instances the associate may work on jobs in which the client is not his but the company's. In such instances his split of the gross profit will be smaller than when he has brought the client in himself, usually ranging from 40 to 20 percent.

To the young designer the associate basis is an excellent platform from which to launch a career, since a tremendous amount of valuable know-how can be gained by working with one's own clients, with the help of experienced designers and a functional business operation. It is the natural place to start for the designer who has contacts but doesn't know how to make the first formal and financial steps to develop these contacts—or if he or she has contacts but no capital. Subject, of course, to the operating methods and policies of the firm, the associate enjoys immeasurably greater freedom and opportunity than an employee. The mutual rewards of association can be enormous to all concerned. To the established firm association offers a means of bringing in new talent and new clients, of changing a fading image, of keeping up with changes in taste and demand.

C. PARTNERSHIP

Webster defines partnership as "Two or more persons engaged in the same business enterprise and sharing its profits and risks." The partnership form of business is a possibility for two or more designers who feel that they would make a good team, complementing and reinforcing each other in talent and experience. The idea of partnership occurs naturally where two designers have a compatible esthetic bent but different strengths in terms of the ability to attract clients, negotiate in the market, and handle various technical phases of the work. It also occurs logically where designers feel that they need to share the burden of responsibility, where they feel that being on call and on the job day in and day out, year in and year out, is beyond their endurance. Partnership offers the possibility of relief from one of the great disadvantages of the one-person (or one-principal) company—the necessity to work under pressure without respite for long periods when jobs come in thick and fast.

Two or more can share the capital risks, as well as the responsibilities, divide their time "on duty," and exchange ideas; two brains can be better than one. Because of its very simplicity and the obvious appeal of its advantages, the partnership form is often plunged into without sufficient consideration of its disadvantages.

THE DISADVANTAGES AND HAZARDS OF PARTNERSHIP

Responsibility for the Actions of the Partner. The partnership firm as a whole and all the individual partners are generally responsible for the actions of each and every partner. Whatever any partner does in business, whatever promises he makes to clients or to the trade, whatever papers he signs are generally binding on the firm and on each partner together and separately. Whatever damages, losses, mistakes, or lapses he may bring on by omission or commissions are not just the problems of the miscreant alone but of the innocent partner or partners as well.

Unlimited Liability. As in the individual form of company, members of a partnership are personally liable for the financial effects of the business, and there is no limiting these liabilities solely to the assets of the partnership. In the event of insolvency, the creditors can proceed against the assets of the partnership—and the personal assets of its members. Whatever losses are incurred by an irresponsible partner become, as stated above, liabilities against the other partner or partners. The point is that these liabilities are usually unlimited.

With that consideration in mind the choice of a partner is no light matter. However, even if all partners are scrupulous in their dealings with each other and perform their work to the best of their ability, the unlimited liability feature of the partnership form remains a serious potential hazard and disadvantage, for losses can and do occur through innocent misjudgment and even through sheer bad luck. Whatever the cause of the loss in a partnership—as in an individual form—the designer runs the risk of losing more than just business assets.

Income Tax Disadvantages. The partnership form of business exposes the partners to the same possibility of income tax disadvantages as the individual form does. The tax laws regard partners as individuals, and the profits of a partnership are taxed as individual income. Federal income tax requires that the income which each partner earns as his share of the profits of the partnership be added to his "other source of income" in his personal return, raising the total taxable income to a higher possible figure and subjecting that figure to an escalated tax rate—to a higher possible tax rate. As in the case of the individual form, the designer contemplating the organization of a partnership should have a competent business counselor estimate the personal income taxes he would have to pay for a given income and compare that with the taxes he would pay if he organized the company as a corporation.

Simple as the partnership form may appear, it nevertheless requires the formation of a business vehicle, and there are definite formalities involved that should entail the services of an attorney. Competent legal counsel will cover all facets of a properly drawn agreement and also make sure the new enterprise conforms to existing local legal requirements and necessary registrations. It is imperative that the partnership form should not be entered into without this partnership agreement. Among the pertinent factors that the partners must decide and include in the legal agreement are

1. Capital contributions
2. Share of the profits
3. Use of drawing accounts
4. Definition of responsibilities
5. Methods of dissolving the partnership in the event of:
   a. Unilateral decision to withdraw
   b. Mutual agreement to dissolve
   c. Retirements
   d. Death

Before deciding to draw up a partnership agreement, the parties involved should consider:

1. Do you know and understand your future partner?

2. Can you mesh as personalities under the pressures of work over a long period?

3. Will each partner carry a fair share of the burdens of management and work?

4. Will each partner bring in a fair share of business?

5. Are the partners reasonably similar in esthetic bent and general level of professional proficiency?

6. Have you thoroughly studied the disadvantages and hazards of partnership?

D. THE CORPORATE FORM OF DOING BUSINESS

It has probably occurred to you that in discussing certain disadvantages of the individual and partnership forms of business, we have suggested that the corporate form may offer relative freedom from these disadvantages and that it should be seriously considered by a designer who intends to practice. Even before defining it, we must point out that almost everywhere the corporate form *is* a possible alternative to the individual form and the partnership.

By definition a corporation is "an association of individuals, created by law, having a continuous existence independent of its members, and powers and liabilities distinct from those of its members." But remember: you can legally have a corporation consisting of only *one* individual (in most states) or a corporation of *two* (or of course more) individuals. What counts is not the number of people who own a corporation but the fact that the corporation is a *separate entity;* legally and financially it exists apart from its owners. Herein lie the all-important differences between an individual form or partnership and a corporation.

Organizing a corporation entails legal formalities. An attorney should be retained since the procedures and the structure of the corporation must conform with the laws of the state in which the company is incorporated. Professional guidance should be sought when appropriate for the preparation of a stockholders' agreement among the stockholders and the corporation. These kinds of agreements might include among other things the following issues:

1. Restrictions on the sale of stock by stockholders to third parties.

2. Rights and obligations of withdrawing stockholders.

3. Consequences of the death of a stockholder.

4. Control and management over the operations of the business.

These are just a few of the matters that should be discussed with counsel so that the business operations are not adversely affected at some later date by a controversy created by disputing shareholders.

ADVANTAGES OF THE CORPORATE FORM

1. Limited Liability. The most important advantage of the corporate form is that it limits the liability of the stockholder to the amount invested by him, and generally, the stockholder is not personally liable for financial losses resulting from the operations of the business beyond—again—the sum invested by him except for certain taxes and other obligations that the law imposes personal responsibility for. However great the company's debts, creditors cannot, generally, go beyond the assets of the corporation because the corporation and the owners of the shares of stock are *not* one and the same entity. The debts of the corporation are *not* the debts of the designer.

Heed, however, must be taken by the designer who seeks to take advantage of the corporate format. The designer must remember to maintain, in the course of his or her business operations, strict corporate formality. For example, a separate bank account or accounts must be maintained for the corporation. Contracts must be entered into in the corporate name. These are just a few examples of formalities that must be strictly followed.

We have on several occasions witnessed a designer who made the effort to incorporate, but then lost the advantage of limited liability offered by the corporate structure by entering into contracts in his name alone and ordering merchandise from trade sources in his name

alone. The designer mistakenly thought all he needed to do to obtain the advantage of limited liability was to incorporate.

Because of limited liability the corporate form is exceptionally well suited to the interior design field. In selecting the appropriate business form, the designer must realize that the business of interior design involves not only the usual risks of debt that threaten every business enterprise, but also the higher degree of risk that arises in the handling of a client's funds and goods and in the purchasing, processing, and transporting of goods from trade sources.

2. Income Tax Benefits. Income tax laws treat the corporation as a separate entity subject to its own tax rates. In many cases the effective corporation tax rate that applies may be appreciably lower than the rate that would apply if the company's profits were included in the owner's individual tax return. For the purpose of illustration, let's consider this example. If the base corporate tax is 16 percent on net income up to $25,000 and if an individual is in a personal income tax bracket above 16 percent, he can to an extent shelter the income from his design firm by operating it as a corporation, subjecting its profits to the current flat 16 percent—instead of the tax rate that would be assessed against the income if he were operating his firm as an individual company. In any case a professional tax accountant should be consulted to analyze the comparative tax picture of the firm as a corporation versus another business structure.

Current tax regulations have eased somewhat the problem of surplus accumulation and the mandate to declare dividends—which in the case of small businesses may sometimes create burdens counterbalancing the tax advantage of the corporate form. This burden is now being eased to a great extent, and you may easily check with tax counsel as to the current "allowable earnings credit" before the need to declare dividends—to avoid a double tax on dividends and profits.

The designer's tax counselor should also investigate another tax innovation: the use of the Subchapter S Corporation allows the profits or losses of the corporation to be taxed at personal income tax rates, while still retaining the corporate structure and the corporate advantage of limited liability. This can be an advantage for young firms that may possibly suffer losses in the first years of operation.

3. Issuance of Stock for Capital. If the firm needs additional capital, corporation law allows the managers to attract investment money by issuing and selling shares of stock.

4. Immortality. The corporation's identity and activity are unaffected by the death or disability of any stockholder.

5. Superior Profit-Sharing and Pension Benefits. The benefits from profit-sharing and pension plans that can be derived under corporate regulations are significantly superior to those allowed in individual form companies or partnerships. This is another obvious avenue for the designer's financial counselor to investigate.

In summary the corporate form has the advantage of limited liability, which should be stressed as the overriding consideration. The operations of a design practice incur liabilities even in a corporation, but the creditors (except certain preferred creditors in special cases) cannot seek reimbursement from the personal assets of the individual stockholders. Since the ordering of goods, the handling of the client's funds, and the processing of the client's own goods create never-ending opportunities for high damages and losses—and since interior designers are apt to pay more attention to esthetic than to business problems—they should use any umbrella that offers protection from the hazards of operating in the field. The corporate organization form is one of the biggest and the best umbrellas available.

The disadvantages of the corporate form lie in the formal technicalities and costs of incorporating, prescribed formalities to be followed during the existence of the corporation, and certain state franchise and stock taxes.

Location and Nature of the Business

Having decided in what area of design to specialize and which business formation to choose, the budding designer-businessperson must decide on the location and nature of his or her workplace. Depending on his chosen field, his capital, the geographic and economic characteristics of his community, and the image he wants to project, the designer may choose to set up his firm as:

A. A home studio

B. A business office

C. A retail establishment

The advantages and disadvantages of each are detailed below.

A. THE HOME STUDIO (OR HOME OFFICE)

The location most beginners think of first is to set aside a part of his or her residence for business. It should be reviewed in light of the following advantages and disadvantages:

1. Advantages
   a. Capital required is minimal, with practically no outlay for rent, decor, furnishings, equipment, and continuing overhead.
   b. If tastefully furnished, the designer's residence can serve as a showcase for his or her talents.
   c. It creates an aura favorable to a practice specializing in residential interiors.
   d. It solves certain special personal situations where the designer finds it difficult to absent him- or herself from the home; an obvious example is a woman with small children who either cannot afford or doesn't want to leave them in the care of others.
   e. It may be the only possible location in small communities where suitable business premises do not exist.
   f. It may provide an ideal setting for the personal nature of designer-client relationships that are typical of certain small communities.
   g. From a tax viewpoint, a portion of the expenses of a home studio may be proper deductions as business rent. These expenses must be assessed by the designer's accountant, because the Internal Revenue Service has set up a series of guidelines for determining this deduction.

2. Disadvantages
   a. Since the image of a home' studio does not sit well with business executives, the home studio is not desirable if the designer wants to do nonresidential interiors. Business executives prefer to work with other business executives.
   b. The home studio looks suspiciously unbusinesslike to trade sources. Designers in major market areas are apt to find that trade sources will not welcome designers who appear to be involved in purchasing for themselves and their personal friends.
   c. The constant flow of clients, deliverymen, and employees can disrupt the private premises, and if areas subjected to traffic are inadequate, the result will be unwieldy, irritating operations.
   d. In many communities zoning laws prohibit the use of a residence for business purposes.

B. BUSINESS OFFICE

The successful operation of a business often depends upon the facade it presents to its clients. There is no question that a design office located in a good business area gives the impression of a sound and businesslike organization, particularly in metropolitan centers. This kind of setup gives potential clients a feeling of security and prevents them from speculating that the business is a part-time avocation.

The location of the office depends on conditions in the community. In cities where trade showrooms are centralized in a specific locality, it makes sense for the designer's office to be nearby, saving him or her time and money in covering the market. If no trade showroom center exists, then obviously the factors to be considered are convenience to clients or potential clients and the attractiveness of the neighborhood.

Rental cost should be analyzed in relation to overall operating expenses and to the projected income with which the designer expects to pay expenses. The lease should be reviewed by legal counsel so the designer can be apprised of his or her rights and possible liabilities. For example, leases often contain various escalation clauses (based on the landlord's increase in taxes, fuel costs, and operating expenses) that increase the designer's rental fees.

It is also important for the designer to analyze how much cash is needed if the space will have to be altered and that needed to obtain essential furnishings and equipment. It is poor business judgment to bite off more than you can chew.

C. RETAIL ESTABLISHMENT
In many suburban and rural communities, small home furnishings shops are the most common settings for a design service, and for obvious reasons. The shop's open door naturally attracts potential clients. The retail sale of furnishings and accessories provides the designer with an income base and covers at least part of the overhead. Even in larger communities opening a shop is in certain ways the path of least resistance for a designer who wants to get started, because many people who are still unsophisticated about professional interior design service and timid about seeking it will step into a shop without hesitation. If the designer-entrepreneur can win the shopper's confidence, he or she may develop a future client.

It is necessary to add that running a shop is a business in itself. The traffic patterns and economic conditions of the location have crucial bearing on the designer's chances for success. And the "retail establishment" designer needs

enough working capital to set up the shop and inventory a reasonable stock of furnishings and accessories. The amount of the designer's capital will be a determining factor in how much credit manufacturers and trade sources will extend to him or her.

CHAPTER 5

Securing Essential Counsel and Assistance

On plunging into practice, the neophyte will be confronted with problems beyond his ken, with decisions beyond his experience. Moreover, the young designer may be unaware of the very existence of issues and problems that must be addressed. As a rule this will occur not in the area of design but in the business aspects of his or her practice, since the business world can be a bewildering maze to the uninitiated. Even in the area of design the young member of the profession will, however, occasionally find himself in situations that call for competence not in his own but in some related field—in some profession such as architecture, landscape architecture, or engineering—or in some technical specialty such as lighting, heating and air-conditioning, plumbing, and so forth.

It is a cardinal rule in business that unknown territory should never be explored without a competent guide—a professional or specialist in *that* territory. It takes a shrewdness to know one's own limitations and insight to respect professionalism in fields other than one's own.

The self-deluding amateur who insinuates himself into the trade showrooms and who wastes time, energy, and money in the pathetic game of "getting it wholesale"—that is, avoiding the expense of engaging a professional interior designer—is an excellent example for the inexperienced interior designer to bear in mind when he or she is tempted to cut corners by doing without professional advice. It is unrealistic. It invariably costs much more in the end. Retaining professional counselors is the first step in launching a practice.

As discussed in Chapter 3, the accountant and/or attorney should be consulted before the practice is set up on the question of the most advantageous business formation for the company—individual form, partnership, or corporation—based on an estimate of its effects on taxes and liabilities.

THE ACCOUNTANT

The way business is conducted throughout the world today, it is practically impossible for any business—no matter how small—to operate without the services of a qualified accountant. In a small- or medium-sized firm the accountant is not likely to be a full-time employee but a consultant, though the firm may employ a bookkeeper or even a bookkeeping staff. The fact to understand is that the accountant is much more than a keeper of records or a sender of bills. In addition to the traditional functions of maintaining and interpreting properly kept records, the accountant is an indispensable management consultant and tax advisor—and is becoming more so each year.

At the outset the accountant should be consulted on the crucial question of the amount of capital that will be required for the business venture contemplated. Too many designers waste years building a reputation and setting the stage for operations that are bound to die of attrition before they develop sufficiently to show a profit—simply because they have underestimated the operating capital required. Accountants experienced in the interiors field can give invaluable advice on how much money will be needed to secure necessary credit for stock and other costs, depending on the nature of the firm, the practice, and the community.

The accountant will organize the bookkeeping records and the office procedures and systems necessary for an intelligent control of the flow of operations. He or she will register the new company with the necessary federal, state, and local taxing authorities, so that compliance with the multitude of necessary taxes is assured. He or she will prepare or supervise the preparation of the various tax returns and schedule them for timely filing.

It is necessary to point out that among the various taxes that interior designers face, the sales tax is likely to pose the most problems. If the designer's company is in a state or community where sales taxes are levied, it is of utmost importance that the accountant properly advise the interior designer about the rules governing the imposition or exemption of the tax on the various services performed. This subject is treated in detail in Chapter 18.

As the business gathers momentum, the accountant should be called upon for periodic financial statements and analysis of such statements. This will give the interior designer an intelligent review of the financial results of past operations—and guidance for the future. The accountant will relate past income and operating overhead and will be in a position to project overhead requirements for the future to determine when and if changes in the fee structure might be desirable and how fast the operation should expand or contract.

LEGAL ADVISOR

Legal counsel should be retained to set up a new business in accordance with the law. After that the need for legal counsel will continue as legal decisions and formalities arise from time to time. If the new business is to be a partnership or corporation, an attorney should be retained to draw up the necessary legal documents. If the business is to be operated as an individual form company, an attorney should be consulted about the legal limitations and form of operating under an assumed name and about the problems of unlimited liabilities.

You should seek legal guidance before signing a lease for business premises. An improper or misunderstood lease can wreak considerable damage on the finances or operations of a firm. There are related problems to be considered even if the firm is to be operated from the designer's residence and no leases are necessary, for zoning laws and restrictions must be checked to make sure that the designer's operations will not violate the law.

BANKING FACILITIES AND CREDIT LISTINGS

The new business should arrange for banking facilities close to the office. The bank manager will be most helpful in setting up a commercial account. Such an account should be maintained only for the business and should not be mixed up with personal deposits and disbursements. The initial capital deposit should be big enough to give the business an appearance of stability, for the bank may be called by trade sources for credit information about the designer. Conversely, the bank can give the interior designer invaluable credit information about his own new clients.

It is virtually impossible for a business to operate without obtaining credit terms from trade sources, so it is advisable to register with the leading credit agencies. Trade sources rely on credit agency reports and listings in determining the amount of credit they will advance to the interior designer. One of the following three should carry a listing on the company:

1. Allied Board of Trade, which functions as a clearing house of credit information about interior designers.

2. Lyon Furniture Mercantile Agency, which is best suited for interior designers who operate retail shops.

3. Dun and Bradstreet, a leading national credit agency.

As previously noted, the firm's accountant is the person best qualified to prepare credit registrations, since the financial status of the business is indicated, along with other pertinent facts.

INSURANCE COUNSELOR

A reputable insurance counselor should be retained to survey the potential hazards to which the interior design firm may be subject. It then becomes the counselor's responsibility to provide an insurance program for protection against such eventualities. Obviously the scope of the program will vary with the size and complexity of the firm.

Proper insurance coverage is of utmost financial importance should an unforeseen casualty occur. Unnecessary and improper coverage can be expensive. In view of its importance, the subject is treated in greater detail in Chapter 27.

TECHNICAL ADVISORS AND
COLLABORATORS IN RELATED FIELDS

In developing certain interior design jobs, the designer may face problems that he or she is professionally, technically, or legally unqualified to solve because they are beyond the scope of interior design. Not all designers are alike in the range of their technical know-how, of course. There is considerable variation in the curricula of design schools, and no designer is given the same opportunities to learn from experience as any other, so that the cutoff point of competence will vary with each individual. But there is hardly any designer who will not find him- or herself at that point at one time or another. He or she will face a job calling for architectural working drawings or electrical duct layouts, ventilation system details or specifications for heavy construction, or a general coordination of many different technical facilities that are definitely beyond his or her capabilities. It is necessary to establish working contacts with architects, electrical engineers, air-conditioning and ventilating experts, and good general contractors so that he or she will have collaborators ready when needed. The designer must restrict his or her activities to those properly performed by an interior designer and should inform the client when the services of other professionals are required.

PART 2

Carrying a Job through and Charging for It

Initial Contact with the Client

How the potential client comes upon the designer to whom he or she wants to offer a job—or where and how designers and clients find each other—is beyond the scope of this book. Here we are concerned not with whether the potential client was charmed by the designer's work or awed by his fame nor why he decided to seek out *that* particular designer—but *what happens next*. If the job hanging in the balance is to be successful for everyone involved, this stage is crucial, and we cannot overemphasize this phase of the project. Our experience proves that a thoughtless approach to this phase produces more problems in the designer-client relationship than any other factor. A great deal depends on how the designer handles the first interview or interviews. That preliminary contact when the client broaches the possibility of the job should be used by the designer to obtain some very essential information without which the designer is wholly unable to determine, among other things, whether to accept the project, how to work, and how to charge.

Regardless of whether a designer and client are meeting for the first time or are already acquainted with one another, the client's first expression of interest in having the designer do a job sets a familiar series of events into motion. The designer should see to it that these events follow a fairly standardized pattern and include certain procedures—beginning with the first formal interview about the job.

1. THE FIRST FORMAL INTERVIEW

This initial meeting should ideally be in the designer's studio, the setting which he has created for himself, among the effects and trappings that show his professionalism, facilities, talent, and artistic concerns. If instead the first interview turns out to be an inspection of the client's home by the designer, the designer must ask him- or herself whether to charge for the time and cost of traveling. Many designers do not charge for the first interview if it takes place at the client's home in the belief that this expense should be charged off as one of the costs

of developing potential sales. Even if the cost is rationalized in that way, it is our opinion that a visit to a place far from the designer's base should be charged for at a flat hourly or per diem rate sufficient to cover both the time and travel expense.

2. THE QUESTION OF RAPPORT

Rapport is important in all areas of interior design, but it is absolutely crucial in residential work, where the very nature of the task requires that the designer spend a great deal of time in personal contact with the client. Versatility and flexibility are desirable qualities in interior designers, some of whom can do an amazing variety of work for many different kinds of clients. Nevertheless there are occasions when the obvious differences between clients and designers in such matters as taste, temperament, manners, and ideas about styles of living are so great that they are bound to disagree about design. In nonresidential work it may be enough for the designer to stay within a specified mode or style and meet specified functional requirements in design, while correctly carrying on the business transactions to insure that the job proceeds satisfactorily. But in residential work it is important that the very first meeting indicate strong rapport between client and designer. Without actually falling in love with each other, they should understand each other and be able to get along—and there has to be definite esthetic rapport as well. If the initial interview indicates mutual irritation, the designer should seriously consider the consequences of taking on the client. It may be wiser not to go on.

3. THE DESIGNER'S ABILITY TO SELL HIMSELF

Being able to promote himself is essential if he wants a firm of his own. From the first the designer must not only inspire confidence, but give the client tangible clues that he is likely to fulfill the client's conception of what he wants. Even if the client has seen a little of the designer's work, he or she may not grasp that the designer can do many things. That's why it is important to have pictures of completed work to show. Sketches are better than nothing. Although black-and-white photographs are more convincing than sketches, they fail in the important requirement of showing color. Models are very impressive indeed, but designers in the residential field have relatively little occasion to prepare them. Color photographs, and above all color slides, are ideal. A library of stereoscopic color slides can include many beautiful interiors and can be stored in a small space. When projected, they can give an effective idea of the three-dimensional reality, size, and color.

As will be pointed out in Chapter 8, Letters of Agreement, it is important that you obtain your client's consent to photograph the completed premises and use these photographs for promotional purposes.

There is no substitute, of course, for showing actual installations, but it takes valuable time and is not always easy to arrange if the occupants resent intrusions on their privacy or are not maintaining the space as designed. But where a big job is hanging in the balance, a guided tour may be essential to enable the client to make up his or her mind.

4. THE DANGER OF OVERSELLING

At the first meeting the danger of overselling is real if the designer is eager to get the job and quick to develop ideas. Often enthusiastic designers have rushed into long and detailed descriptions of their proposed solutions immediately, going so far as to sketch furniture layouts, put together color schemes and fabric and paint samples, and show photographs of furniture, drapery treatments, carpeting, and other elements. If the potential client is on a brain-picking expedition, the designer has served him or her well. Many "clients" have been known to interview designer after designer, collecting a vast fund of ideas and suggestions. And many have been known to transform themselves into instant decorators, doing

their own buying and installing, following the suggestions stolen from their unwary victims. The experienced designer goes just so far and no further in making specific suggestions to a client who has not yet retained him or her and is still just shopping around.

5. DEFINING THE SCOPE OF SERVICES

Determining the scope of services is one of the important things to accomplish in the initial meetings. The designer should not accept a job, discuss design concepts in detail, quote a fee, or state the compensation arrangement without knowing what the job entails. To know that involves knowing the attitude, desires, and needs of the client. This can only be developed through initial discussions with the client and the development of an analysis of scope of services.

Without an understanding of the variables of both the client and the job, the designer might easily accept jobs that are not for him, and if he does, he is risking his reputation as well as his pocketbook. The following chapter, Analysis of Scope of Services, points out the various items that should be reviewed during the initial contact with a potential client.

6. DEFINING THE FIRM'S FINANCIAL METHODS

Another thing that needs to be taken care of at the initial interview is defining the financial methods the firm will use. The potential client should be advised of the firm's business procedures and its methods of charging. The points to be covered include the letter of agreement, the retainer, the deposits required for purchase orders, the method and timing of billing, and the fee basis. It is as important for the client to have as much information as possible about the designer and his or her business methods as it is for the designer to know as much as possible about the potential client.

7. THE NEW PROJECT CHECKLIST

The checklist shown on page 34 is helpful in

New Project Check List—Residential

Company Name

Date _____

Designer _____

Client _____   Husband _____   Wife _____
            (Last Name)   (Initial)   (First Name)   (First Name)

Street _____   Install Address _____

City & State _____   City & State _____

Telephone _____   Telephone _____

Business Affiliation _____   Referred by _____

Design Information _____

Areas Involved — Scope of Services _____

_____

_____

_____

Type of Design Desired (Style, Color, etc.) _____

_____

_____

Husband's Business or Profession _____

Children (No., Age, Sex) _____

Allergies or Handicaps _____   Pets _____

Social Activities (Describe) _____

_____

Estimated Budget _____

Credit Check _____

Deposit or Retainer _____

Fee Basis _____

_____

Expenses Reimbursed _____

Installation Date Requested _____

Travel Directions _____

_____

Other Comments _____

_____

Form No. 1 (To obtain forms, see page 4.)

collecting and clarifying some of the essential information about the client. Interior design is not a simple sales transaction, but a series of personal interactions and communications between two parties who are producing a complex work of art—an intimate personal environment for an individual or group of individuals. Information can be entered on this sample form during the initial interview.

Analysis of Scope of Services

The term *analysis of scope of services* has such import that it should be posted prominently in every interior design office and planted firmly in the mind of every designer. The nature, extent, and types of services that can be rendered are so broad that without knowing what a client wants and/or needs, there cannot be a logical approach to making meaningful decisions as to accepting an assignment, the design concept, the fee or compensation base, and most importantly the contractual relationship.

An orderly and precise development of the scope of services should be the basis on which the designer will accept or refuse the assignment and, if accepted, will give the designer a firm grasp of the elements necessary to begin the job process. This approach must incorporate two aspects:

1. The client's views of the various elements.

2. The designer's requirements for developing a successful esthetic and financial result.

The initial discussions with a potential client must give the designer the following information:

1. What the client wants.

2. What the client needs.

3. The ability of the client to pay for what he wants and/or needs because:

    a. What a client wants, he may not need.

    b. What a client needs, he may not want.

    c. Perhaps what he really wants is what he can pay for.

This initial analysis will give the designer the basic information needed to develop the potential design concept, the breadth of the project, and the budget base. However, if the potential client has an unrealistic approach to the design concept, to the budgetary requirements, to the desired installation date, to services required, or even to professional interior designers in general, this is the time for the interior designer to inform the client to adjust his or her thinking or back off.

Once the designer has a firm handle on what the client wants, he or she can begin to develop the following required parameters:

A. Design concepts

B. Service requirements

C. Budget requirements

D. Fee and compensation base

E. Terms and conditions of the contractual relationship

Each one of these points will be discussed in detail below.

A. DESIGN CONCEPTS

1. Is the concept within the designer's capabilities or natural direction of his or her talent?

2. Is the client's concept in the realm of reality or so far out that a responsible solution cannot be found?

3. Is the project too large (will you get in over your head)?

4. Is the project too small, with minor compensation, or will there be future work?

5. Are you aware of the client's esthetic preferences or aversions that will
    a. Expedite the design concept development time.
    b. Control market research and shopping time.
    c. Reduce negative reactions from the client.
    d. Avoid costly adjustments.

Included in this chapter on the facing page is an abbreviated checklist guide for developing client's preferences or aversions.

B. SERVICE REQUIREMENTS

The designer must be aware of the various outside services that the project may require and the impact of such requirements on:

CLIENT PREFERENCE CHECKLIST

PERIODS

Contemporary_____

Traditional_____

Formal_____

Informal_____

Eclectic_____

Other_____

COLOR

Light_____

Pastels_____

Dark_____

Monotone_____

FABRICS & WALLPAPERS

Prints_____

Florals_____

Geometrics_____

Plaids_____

Stripes_____

Animals_____

Other_____

FLOOR COVERING

Ceramic tile_____

Vinyl tile_____

Carpet_____

Rugs_____

Wood_____

Other_____

WALLPAPER OR PAINT

List areas_____

AREAS FOR TV

List_____

TELEPHONE LOCATIONS

List_____

LIGHTING

Track_____

Recessed_____

Lamps_____

Chandeliers_____

Other_____

SPECIAL AREAS

Bar_____

Game table_____

Other_____

ACCESSORIES

Lucite_____

Glass_____

Bronze_____

Brass_____

Chrome_____

Wood_____

Other_____

1. The budget base.

2. The compensation base.

3. The geographical availability of such services.

Such services fall into the following categories:

1. Architectural services
2. General contractor's services
   a. Construction
   b. Carpentry
   c. Plumbing, etc.
   d. Landscaping
   e. Heating, ventilation, and air conditioning
   f. Availability of local contract sources

C. BUDGET REQUIREMENTS

If the client has a predetermined budget, is it realistic? If it is not, the designer should inform him or her at once. Remember: in the anxiety of obtaining a job, do not make a promise you won't be able to keep. If a client does not have a budget, help him or her develop one. You should study Chapters 13 and 14 for a full description of the various elements involved in the client's budget.

D. FEE AND COMPENSATION BASE

There are many fee basis and compensation methods to select from, and determining which to use or which to combine depends on finding ones that are fair to both the client and the designer. The compensation base should be commensurate with the services, talent, and time involved in each individual project—it should never be a *rote* decision. By analyzing the scope of services, the designer should obtain the information needed to determine his compensation base and discuss this phase in an intelligent fashion at the initial meetings with his client. If the client's attitude, the extent of the project, or both are such that the compensation will be inadequate, don't take the job. Never rely on "hope and prayer" that you can correct the situation as the job progresses or,

worse, at the end of the job. The various fee bases and their applications are detailed in Chapter 10, Methods of Determining Fees and Compensations.

D. TERMS AND CONDITIONS OF THE CONTRACTUAL RELATIONSHIP

The interior design profession places strong emphasis on having the conditions and arrangements of a design project in writing. Because the analysis of scope of services brings to light and identifies the salient facts around which the project will revolve, the more extensive the analysis, the more inclusive becomes the letter of agreement and the less possibility of misunderstandings. Guidance on the rationale for and development of a letter of agreement or a contract, together with explanatory material, is described in detail in Chapter 8, Letters of Agreement.

Sound business practices demand that if an interior designer is to successfully complete a project, he must know the various elements involved *before* he accepts the project, *before* he enters into a letter of agreement, and *before* he begins to work on the job. Failure to develop the scope of services as a preliminary step is an open invitation to confusion, unnecessary costs, and perhaps the unpleasantness of litigation.

As an additional guide in establishing checklists, refer to Harry Siegel's book, *Business Guide for Interior Designers*, published by the Whitney Library of Design. This book contains a practical checklist for analyzing the various conditions of a design project, together with related clauses for a letter of agreement.

CHAPTER 8

Letters of Agreement

Just mention the word "contract" to a designer and you may very well witness a significant increase in blood pressure. The concern and apprehension a designer may feel when having to present a contract to a prospective client, let alone prepare it, is both commonplace and understandable. This aversion to legal documents extends beyond the field of interior design. It can be seen in many aspects of everyday life. Yet, the process of contract preparation and presentation to a client should not be such an anxiety-producing event.

In general, those designers who really do not understand the purpose, need, and mechanics of a contract are most vocal in opposing its use. Those who understand the need, the purpose, the mechanics, and, most importantly, the analysis that one must go through in the course of preparing it are those who are most comfortable with its use and who recognize its benefits and limitations.

So that there is no misunderstanding wherever the term *letter of agreement* is used in this book, this letter is no more or less than a *contract* if the requisite elements are contained in it. Call it a *letter of agreement* or anything else you feel comfortable with. What you label it is not important; what is important is what it contains.

From time to time we have been asked to distinquish those projects where a designer should have a written agreement from those where a written agreement is not needed. This distinction does not exist. *All projects should be covered by a properly drawn written agreement.* Whether the project is residential or nonresidential, whether the project is large-scale or relatively small, they should all be covered by a sensible written agreement. While the terms of agreements may differ depending upon the nature and scope of the project, the need for a written agreement remains ever present.

Given the clear need for a written agreement, how does one go about preparing one? Let us set aside for now the question of who will actually prepare the writing (that is, you or your ad-

visers); the procedure should begin with a thorough analysis of the scope of the project. Because of the extreme importance of this initial phase, a new chapter has been added to the book, Chapter 7, entitled Analysis of Scope of Services. This would be an opportune time to reread this new chapter. Until you are armed with sufficient information to analyze the nature of the project, the compensation arrangement best suited for that particular project, and other pertinent matters, put down your pencils because you are not ready to prepare the agreement.

While there is no one form of agreement that can be successfully used in every project, there are, however, certain concepts that weave throughout most residential agreements. They may be broadly outlined as follows:

1. Identity of the parties.
2. The design areas involved in the project.
3. Specific design services to be rendered by the designer.
4. Specification and purchasing arrangements.
5. Supervision requirements.
6. Compensation arrangements.
7. Collateral matters:
   a. Reimbursement of out-of-pocket expenses.
   b. Disclaimers of designer's responsibilities.
   c. Rights to photograph and publish the project upon completion.
   d. Third-party services.

Each one of these points will be thoroughly discussed below.

1. IDENTITY OF THE PARTIES

The first question that ought to come to mind is, who is the other party to the agreement? In the residential field, what seems like a rather silly question has unfortunately many times given rise to serious problems. When your clients are a married couple and you wish to hold both responsible for their obligations to you, it is appropriate to have both of them named in the agreement and require both of them to sign the agreement.

Unexpected contingencies such as divorce, separation, or death have generated many a headache for a designer. We have witnessed actual situations where, in the midst of residential projects, the designer was advised to cease all activity since the clients were about to separate or obtain a divorce. The designer ought not to be confronted with the problem of determining who is responsible for his or her fee and purchases simply because the clients are at odds. Thus, as a general recommendation where the residential projects involve both a husband and a wife, have both sign the letter.

2. THE DESIGN AREAS INVOLVED IN THE PROJECT

A mistake often made is the failure to specifically define in the letter of agreement the actual areas within the residence where the designer's services are requested. All too often, reference is merely made to "your home at (address)." This statement seems relatively harmless until you consider its possible effects if the client claims that you failed to complete the project. When specific rooms are not identified that the designer is responsible for, the question of which rooms are included in the agreement might have to be determined in court. The easiest way of avoiding this type of ambiguity is to identify in the letter of agreement the specific rooms the designer is responsible for. If the scope of the project should expand to include additional rooms, that can always be covered in a subsequent letter.

3. SPECIFIC DESIGN SERVICES TO BE RENDERED BY THE DESIGNER

The nature and extent of the services a designer may render vary extensively and should be carefully detailed in the letter of agreement. Clients, particularly those who have never worked with a designer before, may not know the various kinds of services that might be per-

formed. By discussing the services with your client and incorporating them in the letter of agreement, not only do you document what your specific obligations are to your client, but you also inform the client of what services you will render as opposed to those services that might be required from third parties in the completion of the overall project. For example, if architectural services are required, a client should be informed and should be advised to obtain the services of an architect directly. Advising the client of the need for these third-party services in advance avoids having the client unhappily surprised at a later date. It is important to remember that third-party services could have a significant bearing upon the overall project budget.

As mentioned before, the nature and extent of services performed by designers in residential projects vary considerably. Some of the more commonly identified services (other than specification, purchasing, and supervision that are discussed later in this chapter) are

a. Initial design studies.

b. Preparation of plans showing internal layout of rooms, with measurements taken or confirmed by the designer.

c. Consultations with the client pertaining to budget and design requirements and preferences.

d. Preparation of drawings illustrating recommended designs for interior layouts.

e. Preparation of drawings and other materials illustrating design concepts, color schemes, floor coverings, wall coverings, ceiling treatments, and window treatments.

f. Preparation of layout plans for movable furniture and furnishings.

g. Preparation of illumination plans showing locations of fixtures and outlets.

h. Preparation of schematic drawings for builtins and closets.

i. Consultations with third parties employed by the client (such as architect or general contractor).

These are but a few of the kinds of services that might be rendered. Of course, each designer will have to consider the requirements of each particular project to properly identify the services to be rendered for that job.

4. SPECIFICATION AND PURCHASING ARRANGEMENTS

More often than not in the typical residential project the designer is called upon not only to specify the decorative merchandise and services required, but to purchase from design sources and resell to the client such merchandise and services. It is crucial that the letter of agreement detail the mechanics of these purchasing arrangements.

The letter of agreement should state that the designer will place orders for goods and services only upon receipt of confirmation for such orders signed by the client and accompanied by the client's check for the required deposit. (The underlying theory of confirmations, their provisions, manner of preparation, and use, together with examples of typical forms, are covered in the next chapter, Chapter 9). Where the designer is working on a list price or cost-plus arrangement, it is appropriate to include in the letter of agreement a statement that all items of furniture, furnishings, and decorative accessories specified by the designer are to be purchased solely through the designer. This protects the designer from the client purchasing directly from suppliers merchandise specified by the designer, thus in effect depriving the designer of his or her compensation. Where the client expresses a desire to purchase merchandise directly, the agreement should specify such arrangements and the manner in which the designer is to be compensated for selecting and specifying the merchandise.

The terms of payment for the merchandise ordered should be clearly described in the letter of agreement. For instance, if your arrangement with the client is that the balance of the purchase price for merchandise ordered is payable when the merchandise is ready for delivery and installation, these terms should be included in the letter of agreement. Whatever the payment terms are, they should be clearly stated so that there is no question at a later date, after the merchandise has been ordered, when payment of the balance due is to be made. The question of when payment is to be made for sales tax, delivery costs, installation charges, and insurance costs should likewise be addressed in the agreement.

5. SUPERVISORY REQUIREMENTS

The extent of supervisory services to be provided by the designer is an issue that has often provoked substantial difficulty between designer and client. Clients, unless they are cautioned otherwise, expect the designer to provide what may be termed, for lack of better words, *general overall* supervision. Unless the designer is prepared to render day-to-day supervisory services, it is extremely important that the letter of agreement limit the supervisory obligations of the designer. The client must understand that the designer's supervisory services are not unlimited. For example, the letter of agreement might state that "the designer is not obligated to render day-to-day supervisory services, but will supervise installation of builtins and final placement of movable furniture and furnishings." Unless the supervisory services are properly defined and limited, the designer may be confronted with extraordinary, burdensome demands that are most difficult to meet.

6. COMPENSATION ARRANGEMENTS

The basis for the designer's charges for services to the client—whether it be a fixed fee, a percentage of costs, an hourly rate, or one that is included within the prices to be charged for goods and services—should be set forth and clearly understood by the client.

The designer's various methods of setting fees and compensations are covered in Chapter 10. A complete letter of agreement will always clearly describe the client's obligations for compensation as to both amount and time of payment. Anything short of that invites dispute.

A few words should be added about the concept of a minimum design fee. Many designers consider it sound business practice to be paid a fee for the initial study and planning of the project that is separate and distinct from any other fee involved in the job. This fee is collected before the work begins, preferably upon execution of the letter of agreement, and is treated as a minimum payment for the designer's services. The size of the fee should be based upon the nature of the job, as well as the amount of time and effort involved. Requesting a minimum design fee, particularly in residential projects, is a procedure well worth considering.

7. COLLATERAL MATTERS

There are many other considerations that should be properly addressed in the letter of agreement that do not conveniently fall within any of the foregoing categories. Such matters, among others, include:

a. Reimbursement of out-of-pocket expenses.

b. Disclaimers of designer's responsibilities.

c. Rights to photograph and publish the project upon completion.

d. Third-party services.

Each of these points will be discussed below as follows.

A. REIMBURSEMENT OF OUT-OF-POCKET EXPENSES

The designer's preliminary analysis of the scope of services and location will indicate whether he or she will incur extraordinary travel expenses, blueprint fees, long-distance telephone charges, or other special expenses required by the site or location. If conditions that may entail special expenses of any kind can arise, it is best for the letter of agreement to spell out the designer's rights to reimbursement and payment arrangements.

B. DISCLAIMERS OF DESIGNER'S RESPONSIBILITIES

Not only is it important to describe the services that the designer will render, but it is equally important to address in a letter of agreement those areas for which the designer specifically disclaims responsibility. Such provisions serve to educate the client about the responsibility of the designer and of the client. For example, the letter may specifically disclaim any responsibility for the designer to either design or modify the design of heating, air conditioning, plumbing, electrical, and other mechanical systems. Under no circumstances should the designer perform any service required by law to be performed by a licensed professional (that is, architect, engineer, landscape architect), and responsibility in such areas should be specifically disclaimed. Each prospective project must be carefully analyzed to identify the specific areas that the designer cannot be held responsible for.

C. RIGHTS TO PHOTOGRAPH AND PUBLISH THE PROJECT UPON COMPLETION

The client should acknowledge, at the outset, the designer's rights to photograph the project when completed and permit the designer to use such photographs for promotional purposes. Since many clients are reluctant to permit photographing of their residence for publication purposes, the designer should agree that such use will be without the client's name and/or address.

D. THIRD-PARTY SERVICES

Where the nature of the project indicates the need for certain third-party services, such as those usually performed by an architect or engineer, the arrangements with these design professionals should be discussed with the client and addressed in the letter of agreement. We suggest that wherever feasible these services be engaged directly by the client under a separate contract, with the understanding that such arrangements with other members of the design team will be coordinated with the agreement between client and designer.

It is virtually impossible to completely identify every provision that a letter of agreement should contain. The intent of this chapter is to make you sensitive to the need to carefully study all the circumstances and requirements of a project before writing a letter of agreement.

What about a printed form contract? Is it advisable to have a standard form of printed contract? In recent years the standard form contract has made its way into use and become accepted in the interior design field. If the designer wishes to use a standard contract, it is most important that the designer truly understand each and every provision contained in it. While many provisions in printed form contracts may apply to a particular project, other provisions may not and necessary provisions may not be included. Since no two design projects are completely similar in scope of services, fee arrangements, or a host of other factors, the standard form contracts should not be used blindly. They must be changed to fit the specific situation by deletion of inapplicable provisions and addition of any requisite terms.

Our experience is that a workable, intelligently drawn, and reasonable letter of agreement frightens neither the designer nor the client. Rather, such an agreement enhances the professional stature of the designer, particularly in the eyes of a business-oriented client. Where a client is unwilling to sign a reasonable letter of agreement, the designer should not undertake the project.

CHAPTER 9

Confirmation of Contract Proposals

In the preceding chapter we referred to "confirmation of purchases" by a designer on behalf of his or her client. These may also be called "confirmations of orders," "purchase proposals," or so forth. Whatever the title, aside from the letter of agreement, they are perhaps the most important documents exchanged between the designer and the client. The confirmation has come into use particularly in the residential field, but it is of equal importance in the nonresidential field, because most designers find it impossible to write an estimate at the inception of the job that will cover *every* item and service, together with its actual cost.

The use of confirmations makes it possible to keep the original letter of agreement or contract relatively simple and concise in language and content, for the confirmations serve in effect as subsidiary contracts that spell out all those details that come up on the job after the original letter of agreement has been written and signed.

Let us examine what a confirmation accomplishes: when a designer selects merchandise or completes the plans or design specifications for custom-made items, it is essential that he or she secure the client's written agreement before proceeding with the purchase or with the order for the work. This is done by delivering to the client some form of written document that completely describes the proposed purchase or custom item in full detail, including the cost. It makes sense then to require that the client, if he accepts the proposal, return a signed copy of it to the designer, signifying his confirmation of the proposal.

If the item has been properly described in the proposal, the client has the right to expect it and to hold the designer responsible for its delivery. If the item delivered is as described in the proposal, the client has no right to refuse to accept it or to refuse to accept liability for the purchase made in his or her behalf. By preparing confirmations for every purchase and order needed for the job, the designer is protected because the client has been fully advised about the nature and cost of each item and has given signed approval of it. So very often have we seen a designer confronted by a client who says, "I didn't want this" or "I didn't order that" or "That sofa is too small" or "That wasn't the color of the fabric that I saw." A signed confirmation that lists the items to be ordered, perhaps with sample color or strikeoff, makes short shrift of such a client's contention.

But there is one additional requirement that must be made before the confirmation on each item is considered complete, and it is crucial: a *deposit* from the client must be returned with the signed confirmation.

It has been pointed out that some designers make it a practice to require a sizable deposit with the signing of the contract. For example, if the proposed budget for the entire job is $10,000, the designer will expect a deposit somewhere in the vicinity of $3,000. This is unquestionably an excellent way to begin a job. However, many clients are reluctant to give this much at the beginning and would much prefer giving deposits as purchasing proceeds. Therefore, since it is an absolute necessity for the designer to adhere to what we call the "deposit principle," there is no better way to proceed than to request that the client pay the deposit for each specific purchase at the same time he or she returns the signed confirmation.

The majority of successful interior designers adhere strictly to the deposit principle in residential practice because:

1. When a client sends a 50 percent payment for an item or service, the designer can be well assured that the client has made up his mind that this is what he wants, so that rejection of delivered goods will be held to a minimum.

2. Obtaining the client's deposit funds will keep the balance of his accounts receivable at a decent level.

3. Few designers have sufficient capital to meet the deposit or payment requirements set in the credit terms of trade sources. Clients' deposits

serve as working capital during the period between ordering for the client and finally collecting from the client.

4. The deposit principle safeguards against excessive losses caused by irresponsible clients. The following example illustrates this point: assume that the designer works on the retail basis and that he or she is purchasing a sofa for the client.

List price	$1,800
Cost to designer (40% off)	$1,080
Deposit requested from client (50% of list price)	$ 900

Should the client default on accepting delivery, the worst that can happen to the designer is that he will lose $180—the difference between his cost of $1,080 and the deposit of $900.

A confirmation can be prepared for the purchase of a single item or more than one. Depending upon the size of the job and the purchasing habits of the designer, it is not unusual to have a sizable volume of paper work in processing the great number of confirmations in a single job. But the benefits of the confirmation system more than make up for the expense and work entailed.

The confirmation should be prepared in triplicate. Two copies are sent to the client with instructions to return one signed copy together with the required deposit to the designer and retain one copy for his or her records. The designer keeps one copy as a record of outstanding confirmations, which is then matched to the signed copy when it is returned by the client. After it has been returned, the confirmation can then be used as a guide for the preparation of purchase orders.

In the confirmation system it is essential to emphasize that purchase orders are *not* sent to vendors *until the confirmation and deposit are returned to the designer's office.* Following this rule will avoid conflicts with trade sources over the cancellation of premature orders. Charges for cancelled orders are difficult to pass on to a client unless the cancellation can be pinpointed directly to the client's own action. If a confirmation of order has been signed and cancellation then follows because the client changed his or her mind, obviously the fault lies with the client. If there is no confirmation of purchase, the client can easily deny that he or she gave the designer a verbal instruction to purchase and thus attempt to avoid any liabilities.

It is important that the designer get his or her client used to the procedure of signing confirmations and remitting deposits. So long as you make the effort to prepare and send confirmations, be sure to follow up and see that it is returned to you, for without its return, signed and with a deposit, it does not fulfill its intended purpose.

The sample forms reproduced in the rest of this chapter may be used to develop a confirmation form suited to the particular needs of your design office. The forms are on pages 46–49. Incidentally, throughout the book, printing on the back of any form is also reproduced. Thus the back of Form No. 2 appears on page 47, following the front on page 46. Exhibits A and B are examples of variations of layouts and physical presentations. However, you should take extreme care in choosing the terms and conditions that you will place on your purchase proposal forms to meet your own specific business requirements. Exhibit C is used to cover any purchase that for some reason must be ordered immediately after having been verbally approved by the client.

A

Proposal Contract

Company Name
Address

To:

We are pleased to submit this agreement for proposed work as follows:

Terms:

50 percent deposit of proposal due on acceptance. Balance due when item is ready for delivery and/or installation.

Name of Company

By: _____

If you wish us to proceed with this work, kindly sign and return copy, retaining original for your record.

Accepted: Date:

_____   _____
                                                  (See Terms and Conditions of Agreement on reverse side)

Form No. 2 (To obtain forms, see page 4.)

Terms and Conditions

1. Orders for articles, materials or contractor's services will not be placed in work until signed confirmation of PROPOSAL CONTRACT is received, together with any required deposit.

2. Prices of materials, articles and contractor's services are subject to change. Before proceeding with order notice of any price increase will be given and confirmation of revised price required.

3. Prices do not include shipping, freight and trucking charges or insurance in transit, all of which will be at Client's expense.

4. Orders approved under this contract are non-cancellable.

5. All orders for materials, articles and contractor's services shall be placed by Designer solely on Client's credit.

6. Prices do not include sales or other applicable taxes.

7. No responsibility is assumed for delays occasioned by failure of others to meet commitments or for any other reason or cause beyond Designer's control.

8. Designs, samples, drawings and specifications shall remain Designer's property, whether or not the work for which they are made be executed.

9. Designer does not guarantee any fabric, material or article against wearing, fading or latent defect, but to extent permitted by law, Client shall have benefit at Client's sole expense in the assertion thereof, of all guarantees and warranties possessed by Designer against suppliers and manufacturers.

10. Furnishing or installing of any or all materials or articles is subject to Designer's ability to obtain the same and to procure the necessary labor therefor and is contingent on strikes, accidents or other causes beyond Designer's control.

11. If Designer is required to render services not contemplated by this agreement or incurs extra drafting or other expenses due to changes ordered by Client or other cause, Designer shall be paid for such extra services and expenses the reasonable value or cost thereof.

A

Form No. 2

B

Confirmation

Company Name
Address

To _____   Date _____

Address _____

_____

Quantity	Details	Unit	Price	Total

Dear

So that we may proceed with this order as soon as possible,
will you please sign the original copy of this confirmation and
return to us, together with your check made payable to ....
.... for the amount of ....
for the 50% deposit required.

Thank you for your valued order and your attention to this
matter.

Terms:
1. AMOUNT OF DEPOSIT_____ BALANCE DUE UPON COMPLETION OF
   THIS ORDER. ORDERS ARE NOT PUT TO WORK UNTIL THIS ACKNOWLEDGMENT
   IS SIGNED AND RETURNED WITH DEPOSIT.
2. All bills payable 5 days after date of delivery.   ACCEPTED:
3. All delivery charges are additional.
4. Subject to Sales Tax and Federal Excise Tax when applicable. _____
                                                                           Signature

Form No. 3 (To obtain forms, see page 4.)

Confirmation

Company Name
Address

C

To _____   Date _____

Address _____

_____

Quantity	Details	Unit	Price	Total
	Dear			
	We have already proceeded with this order, but in keeping with the customary requirements, will you please sign the original copy of this confirmation and return to us, together with your check for the one-third deposit in the amount of			
	Thank you for your valued order and your attention to this matter.			

Terms:
1. AMOUNT OF DEPOSIT_____ BALANCE DUE UPON COMPLETION OF THIS ORDER. ORDERS ARE NOT PUT TO WORK UNTIL THIS ACKNOWLEDGMENT IS SIGNED AND RETURNED WITH DEPOSIT.
2. All bills payable 5 days after date of delivery.   ACCEPTED:
3. All delivery charges are additional.
4. Subject to Sales Tax and Federal Excise Tax when applicable. _____
                                                               Signature

Form No. 4 (To obtain forms, see page 4.)

CHAPTER 10

Methods of Determining Fees and Compensations

How should an interior designer charge for his or her services? On what basis should he arrive at the amount of money due him for each space he designs and executes?

This is the most controversial, most hotly debated, most coyly handled, most misunderstood, and most important problem facing the profession as a whole and the interior designer as an individual—if he wants a reasonable income in exchange for the talent, training, and time he invests in his life's work. Often placed on the defensive, a great proportion of the qualified interior designers in the profession have spent far too much energy trying to prove that they do not make it a habit of robbing the client blind. Instead, they would be well advised to use that energy to develop a rational method of handling the money side of their operations.

The issue of professionalism has in itself clouded the problem of establishing proper fees and compensations. The argument goes that interior designers should stop acting like merchants who sell goods and begin to emulate physicians who charge a flat fee for their skill or musicians who charge for each performance or are engaged by the season. It cannot be denied that the basic commodity sold by the interior designer is complicated with such intangibles as skill and imagination, but no observer can close his or her eyes to the reality that the most "purely" professional fee systems—those based on the flat and hourly fee—have never dominated the field and are not gaining ground in proportion to the rapid growth of the industry. There are good and sufficient reasons why this is so, although the flat and time fee systems work well enough for a small percentage of designers in a small part of their practice.

It is fundamentally irrelevant to equate the method of charging for the design and execution of an interior with the method of charging for an operatic performance simply because both are professional activities. The triumphant tenor who brings down the roof of the Met week after week gets the highest fee per performance. Artistic success equals financial success. Simple.

But many an interior designer who witnesses one esthetic triumph after another finds himself or herself deeper in the red after every job. Artistic success equals financial failure? Obviously not so simple.

What *does* determine whether the designer will or will not make the grade financially?

More than any other factor, the ability to earn a proper financial return—assuming competence as an interior designer—revolves principally upon his or her ability to establish a proper base or method for arriving at fees or compensations.

The bases or methods for computing fees and compensations that are used today have been developed over decades by trial and error. These bases or methods can and do bring adequate financial returns to the designers who know when to use each one and who handle the procedures involved with sound business techniques.

Although this chapter describes the many methods or bases for computing fees, it is up to you to find the right one for each of your jobs. No one method is right for every firm or for every job done by a firm. There can be no standard method because there is no such thing as a standard job. Interior design is a highly unstandardized personal service. Different types of firms provide different types of services to different types of clients in different types of communities in different geographical areas of the country—and *every* variable enters into the fee picture.

To rationally arrive at a fee or compensation base the interior designer must have a thorough grasp of:

A. His or her own operation, overhead, and income requirements.

B. The scope of services for each particular job.

C. What fees and compensation systems are available? How to determine which to use? Knowing the types of fee and compensation bases in use in the field, the designer must learn how to apply the correct base depending upon an analysis of each job.

Each of the three points is discussed in detail below.

A. HIS OR HER OWN OPERATION, OVERHEAD, AND INCOME REQUIREMENTS

Proper bookkeeping records must be maintained so that the designer's accountant can analyze the costs of operation. Professionally interpreted financial statements can show how the costs of operation are related to the income dollar earned and to the labor dollar expended, thus giving a dollars-and-cents picture of the effectiveness of the compensation base used to provide operational overhead and profit. This is not quite as simple as it sounds, because in the interiors field there is generally no steady flow of repetitive business from which to deduce an estimate of operating costs. The interior design firm cannot be compared with a store where customers arrive in a predictable number to purchase specified merchandise upon which specific markups over cost have been placed in order to set retail prices. Nor can the interior design firm be compared with the firm of an accountant or lawyer whose clients are retained on an annual basis. Interior design is non-repetitive. The designer completes an installation for a client without knowing whether he or she will ever see a similar job again. For this reason even the interior design firm that is too small to have a comptroller or financial advisor should retain the services of someone who is in a position to interpret the results of the operation.

Along with the general books two auxiliary types of records should be maintained to accumulate the statistical information most helpful in setting up proper fees and compensations:

1. JOB COST RECORDS

The financial results of every job should be analyzed after its completion: the gross income, costs, time expended, the cost of such expended time, and the net profit. This type of information will measure the financial success of each job, since the designer will be able to relate the amount of time expended to the profits earned, thereby discovering whether he earned $1 an hour or $50 an hour for his efforts. It will show what types of jobs are profitable and what types of jobs should be avoided. It will also indicate what budget base he or she can assume in a job and still end up with a profit. (Very small budgets can result in very small profits, and the designer who takes on too many small-budget jobs may be wasting his or her time.)

2. TIME RECORDS

Since all that the designer actually sells is talent and time, time is a crucial factor. Maintaining accurate time records enables the designer to:

a. Relate time requirements to new jobs he or she is undertaking.

b. Relate time to the progress of current jobs (and therefore to the amount of money for time expended that the job is costing him or her).

c. Relate time to the completed job and the resulting profit. The theory, objectives, and methods of recording time are discussed in greater depth in Chapter 26.

B. THE SCOPE OF SERVICES FOR EACH PARTICULAR JOB

Chapter 7, Analysis of Scope of Services, gives guidelines for the information needed to organize the various facets of the job. Unquestionably this analysis becomes the basic factor in arriving at a proper fee or compensation, because how can the designer quote a fee without analyzing the job first? How can the designer say, "I work on a retail basis" or on a "cost-plus" basis or "for a fee of $ _____ an hour," without first knowing the scope of services he is to perform and the profit he estimates he will make? Yet, unfortunately, this is what many designers do.

First he or she should ask: What does this job entail?

1. Creating a *design concept* with very little purchasing?

2. Producing a *design concept* and completing the *installation, purchasing* all required furnishings, materials, and services?

 3. Will time have to be spent with contractors or architects?

4. Will purchasing be from regular trade sources, or will special construction specifications have to be prepared, necessitating drafting-board time?

5. Are there any unusual job-site problems?

6. Is there a costly travel expense factor?

7. If the job is a long distance from home, what problems and expenses may be presented by local trade sources, tariffs, and freight and delivery charges?

The answers to these questions have a definite bearing on the selection of a compensation base needed to ensure a satisfactory profit.

The client's budget for the job has been mentioned as one of the factors that can be determined through a study of the designer's books. It also has an important bearing on *the scope of services for each job*. Jobs for which the client has a small budget tend to be less profitable than those with a bigger budget. If the budget is smaller than a certain sum, the designer is well-advised to turn down the job. The question is—smaller than what sum?—and the answer is different for every firm. It pays to figure out an accurate answer, and it is necessary to be strict in following the guideline thus indicated. The effect of the client's budget is analyzed in greater depth in Chapter 13.

C. WHAT FEES AND COMPENSATION SYSTEMS ARE AVAILABLE? HOW TO DETERMINE WHICH TO USE?

1. Retail basis

2. Cost plus percentage markup

3. Percentage off retail

4. Flat fee

5. Flat fee plus percentage of costs

6. Hourly or per-diem fee

7. Combination of fees

Each point will be discussed in depth as follows.

1. RETAIL BASIS

The retail basis is best described as the billing for merchandise provided to a client at the list price suggested by trade sources, where such list prices are available. Where list prices are not available, the manufacturer's net price to the designer is marked up to bring the article into the local competitive price range. This markup percentage can generally be between 70 and 100 percent of the manufacturer's net price. *This is unquestionably the most remunerative method of compensation for a designer*, since the cost of goods to the designer at net is substantially lower than the billing price at retail to the client. This method is used by the major interior design firms specializing in residential work where the cost of time involved in the design and installation is not too great and the preponderance of the client's budget is set aside for the purchase of goods and services.

One actual and typical residential installation at retail shows the following figures:

Billing to client	$27,827
Merchandise at cost	$15,298
Construction costs	$ 2,791
Actual cost (exclusive of design time)	$18,089
Gross profit	$ 9,738
% of gross profit to billing price	35%

These figures can be compared with the analysis of another residential job in which labor and construction amounted to a greater proportion of the budget than the furnishing of materials. (Note that there is no *retail price* for construction but simply a markup on the cost of construction.)

Billing to client	$124,095
Merchandise at cost	$ 35,973
Construction costs	$ 58,420
Miscellaneous costs	$ 1,384
Actual cost (exclusive of design time)	$ 95,777
Gross profit	$ 28,318
% of gross profit to billing price	22.8%

Thus we can immediately see that the profit return is affected by the amount of merchandise purchased for the client. Preliminary analysis of the job estimates must be made to indicate the profit return. This profit return should then be further analyzed to determine the estimated amount of design time to be expended on the job.

The designer attempting to work on a retail basis will find that the method is *not* reasonable for a job that consists mostly of custom construction, design unrelated to the selection of merchandise, the preparation of floor plans or layouts, color specifications, the preparation of working drawings, or specifications of construction for architectural details or alterations, with the budget devoted mainly to those items rather than to purchasing furnishings. Thus, for the second example, a design fee should have been added to bring the gross profit up to a reasonable figure of 35 percent.

If the major function of a job is a design unrelated to purchases, then the designer must determine an additional or alternate method of arriving at proper compensation for the proposed work. In this event it would be correct to set a flat fee or hourly charge to compensate for the time allocated to the design phase and add that to the retail billing for the furnishings purchased on behalf of the client.

2. COST PLUS PERCENTAGE MARKUP

With this method, the designer's compensation is determined by adding an agreed percentage to the actual cost of materials purchased for the client. The markup percentages used in the residential field range between 25 and 40 percent. It is a simple method of working with a client, but in its simplicity, it is also the *least remunerative.*

Failure to realize sufficient gross profit with this method can readily be illustrated by the following example:

Manufacturer's list price (sofa)	$1,800
Cost to interior designer (40% off)	$1,080
Designer's markup (25% on cost)	$ 270

To further indicate the profit results of the cost plus percentage markup method, based on the above example:

a 30% markup results in $324 profit

a 35% markup results in $378 profit

a 40% markup results in $432 profit

The designer should compare these results with those of the retail basis:

List price	$1,800
Designer's cost	$1,080
Profit	$ 720

This method may not provide a profit margin required to maintain staff, pay overhead expenses, and properly compensate the designer for time, talent, and effectiveness in producing a better than ordinary installation.

This method of compensation is widely used in many parts of the country by a segment of the design community that is leery of basing its charges on the retail price for fear of competition from hungrier designers and department stores. It is typically used by young designers trying to attract a following. However, the fact must be faced that the cost plus percentage markup basis literally gives away the designer's talent and effort in exchange for a financial return that cannot support his or her business.

If this method *must* be used, it should be in combination with other methods to ensure reasonable compensation for services rendered. Variations that might be considered are

a. Cost plus a percentage markup in addition to an hourly charge (for example, $25 to $50 per hour) for the time spent in developing the design concept, layouts, and consultations.

b. Use the client's budget to determine the extent to which you will use the cost plus system. You can, for example, decide that

Budgets under $10,000 will be charged at retail.

Budgets over $10,000 will be charged at retail on the first $10,000 and a percentage of cost for the rest.

c. Combine cost plus percentage markup and retail by applying the cost plus percentage markup to major items (carpeting, furniture, and so forth) and charging list price for minor cost items (wallpaper and fabric).

3. PERCENTAGE OFF RETAIL

In recent years another method for determining fees has evolved. It is based on the manufacturer's suggested list price less 10 percent. The following example describes the method and the resulting profit:

List price	$1,800
Less 10%	$ 180
Billing price to client	$1,620
Cost to designer	$1,080
Gross profit to designer	$ 540

Comparing this method with the cost plus 25 percent system illustrates a much more favorable profit picture. This method is beginning to be accepted by a segment of the profession. It enables the designer who cannot compete on a full retail basis—because of geographic and economic factors—to offer some incentive of discount to clients while still maintaining a fair

profit for his or her services. The percentage off retail is unquestionably preferable to the cost plus basis.

4. FLAT FEE

The system of charging a sum for all the designer's services on the job and having the client pay trade sources and workrooms for merchandise, workmanship, cartage, and other expenses, which they bill directly to him or her, is based on the theory, summarized at the beginning of this chapter, that all professional people should charge only for their time and skill and not for tangible goods delivered. This is a perfectly valid theory. And a small percentage of interior designers use the flat-fee system in a small percentage of their work.

But in practice this system is extremely difficult to calculate safely, and very few clients are willing to accept it. Its chief application has been in relatively uncomplicated nonresidential jobs and in a few very special and unusual residences for extremely sophisticated clients who are absolutely not typical of the market for the vast majority of interior designers in this country.

The flat-fee system appears simple. In fact, it poses a serious financial hazard, since the designer must guess in advance how much time and work he or she will need to put into the job, calculating the fee as the cost of that time plus a profit. Once having committed himself to a fee, he is bound by the figure. If the job entails more work than he anticipated, he can lose money.

In residential work particularly, it is virtually impossible to project the service and time requirements because of the variables that may develop in the designer-client relationship—the budget, the uncertain temperament of a husband-and-wife client team, the inability of clients to make up their minds about the concepts and items suggested by the designer, and the vagueness of the completion date (since many residential jobs run on a piecemeal basis, with completion one or more years in the future—or sometimes never).

In cases where the potential client expects or requests the flat-fee method, the designer must not quote a figure without carefully analyzing the following factors:

a. A thorough and detailed understanding of the services to be rendered and the specific areas involved, with the proviso that no additional services and areas are to be added.
b. The client's budget must be realistic, since the sums a client spends have a direct bearing on the amount of work the designer will be expected to do. The size of the budget has a direct psychological bearing on the size of the fee the designer can quote.
c. The time required to do the job:
   (1) Development of design concept
   (2) Layouts and specifications
   (3) Renderings or sketches, if required
   (4) Working drawings, if required
   (5) Consultation with clients, architects, contractors, among others
   (6) Supervision of trades, expediting orders from sources
   (7) Shopping time and/or market research
   (8) Supervision of installation
d. A comparison of time spent on prior installations as similar as possible in time factors as the contemplated job is one of the last steps in the calculation. Here is where the designer who has kept job records and has had them systematically analyzed will be in a favorable position to draw valid conclusions about time requirements.

For further discussion of the flat fee, see Chapter 11.

5. FLAT FEE PLUS PERCENTAGE OF COSTS

Since the client's budget has a definite relationship to the calculation of the flat fee, it is imperative that the designer protect himself or herself against an expansion of the budget while the job is in progress. He can do this by quoting a fee and stipulating in addition that he also receive a percentage of all costs over the original budget. This point is related to the role of budget in the preceding paragraphs on flat fee and to Chapter 13, which is devoted entirely to the client's budget. To clarify the point sufficiently here, however, we can give you a simple illustration: If the client has set out to spend a total sum of $15,000—assuming a reasonable $5,000 fee—and later, imagining that he has the designer in his pocket, decides to loosen up and spend $25,000, the designer should not let the original fee stand but insist on negotiating an additional fee calculated as a percentage of the extra expenditure. The percentage may vary from 10 to 25 percent depending upon the original fee and the designer's bargaining position.

6. HOURLY AND PER-DIEM FEES

The time-charge basis for computing a designer's fee is more widely accepted in the nonresidential than in the residential field. Even in the nonresidential field it is more often used in addition to other fee bases than alone. For a thorough understanding of time charges, you should also study Chapter 21, Nonresidential Fees and Compensations, and Chapter 26, Theory, Objectives, and Methods of Recording Time. But for the purpose of this chapter, which is to define and compare all the fundamental bases of establishing fees, it is enough to point out that the time charge is extremely difficult to establish in connection with extensive or complete residential installations. Clients are known to examine, question, and more often than not disbelieve the amount of time required and used by a designer in the completion of a residential job. Even when a designer keeps a time record with painstaking care, there is no possible way to figure out proper compensation when he solves a knotty problem over a cup of coffee or when a spark of creativeness strikes as he tosses through a sleepless night.

However, the hourly or per-diem charge is useful to cover special services rendered by the designer. Examples of services for which this method of computation is logical, effective, and convenient are

a. Initial consultation with a prospective client at the client's residence (to cover travel time and brain-picking).

b. Consultations on specific problems.

c. Travel to markets and shopping time when purchases for clients are minor and the resulting profit markup is insufficient to cover the designer's time. Presumably such travel and market research are undertaken at the client's request in search of items specified for special conditions or whims.

d. Services rendered in collaboration with architects or workers during the construction or alteration of residences.

e. Preparation of specifications and/or working drawings needed for a specific or isolated problem.

Hourly rates vary considerably with the size of the organization, its overhead and operating costs, and the geographical location. Although the subject is covered in greater depth in Chapter 26, we can summarize here that in those design organizations that maintain a staff, the hourly charge for the time of staff members should be no less than three times the actual payroll cost. The principal's time charge in such organizations may vary from $50 to $75 to $100 an hour. Comparatively small firms or individual designers have been using a base hourly charge of approximately $25 to $50. Many designers arrive at their hourly charge by way of information garnered at professional conferences, informal discussions with other designers, or simply picking a number that sounds good. *However, you would be well advised to avoid using arbitrary figures and develop your own thorough analysis of your particular fee requirements in relation to your payroll, overhead costs, competition, the economic conditions of your geographical location, and your own availability.*

You must evaluate the same considerations with flat per-diem charges. *There must be a logical relationship between productive time spent and the factors outlined above, and a sensible and realistic value must be placed on the designer's time.*

7. COMBINATION OF FEES

In any given project, a designer may provide various combinations of services, and so it is logical to use combinations of fees to determine compensation. More and more often, designers are applying this theory of varying compensation bases to a single job and coming up with excellent results. In essence the designer can apply charges for specific services and conditions in addition to the one basic compensation method, be it retail, cost plus, or so on.

The analysis of the job may indicate two or more distinct phases of work. For example, assume that the job requires:

a. Working with the architect.

b. Traveling to major market sources.

c. Purchasing all services and furnishings to complete the design job.

The designer may make the following fee arrangements:

a. Phase I: Hourly rate for time spent with architect.

b. Phase II: Per-diem rate on travel time.

c. Phase III: Retail basis for all purchases.

Or assume that a residential job requires that the designer perform the following:

a. Phase I: Develop the design concept.

b. Phase II: Develop the required budget.

c. Phase III: Purchase all furnishings including custom-designed items.

In this instance the designer might use the following combination of fee arrangements:

a. Phase I: Flat fee or X dollars per room or area.
b. Phase II: Hourly rate or flat fee (this fee is often credited to the client's account if the designer gets the job).
c. Phase III:
    (1) Percentage markup on cost for major items.
    (2) Retail for minor items.
    (3) Markup on cost for custom items or time charges for board time, with client charged actual cost of item.

The use of a combination of fees has become a highly acceptable procedure for both the designer and the client. Properly applied, the designer receives commensurate compensation for the various services performed and the client is aware of the various services provided and their costs.

CHAPTER 11

Approach to the Flat Fee

The subject of flat fees was just discussed in Chapter 10. However, since the flat-fee basis can be difficult to apply and financially dangerous for the uninitiated and uninformed, this chapter will outline how to approach the flat fee, the pitfalls it may entail, and the safeguards that might be applied.

It is important to understand that the flat fee is a valid method of setting a compensation base, and it has most often been identified with the nonresidential field. However, its proper application is possible in every area of the interior design field, and as a matter of fact, it might almost be a necessity under certain circumstances, such as developing design layouts and/or specifying furnishings when the client is taking responsibility for the actual ordering.

TO DETERMINE THE FEE QUOTATION

COMPARE WITH COMPLETED PROJECTS

After the initial meetings with the client have established the specifics of the project, a most reliable guideline for setting a flat fee is *past experience.* The designer who keeps job cost records (as described in Chapter 16) can compare a proposed project with completed projects.

Designers who have completed flat-fee projects in the past should organize individual job records to show:

1. The nature of the job.

2. The areas involved.

3. Total fees billed.

4. Total time costs by employee.

5. Total cost of purchases and services, if available, or client's budget.

6. Total other direct costs incurred and absorbed by the designer.

Proper analysis of these records provides the following valuable reference statistics:

1. The profit on time expended (fees billed minus time costs).

2. The percentage relationship of the fees to direct costs.

3. The percentage relationship of the fees to absorbed job expenses.

Now, given the specifics of the new project, the designer can compare them with past results and make a fee calculation from a sound base.

ANALYZE YEARLY PROFIT RECORDS

Designers who have never worked on a flat-fee basis and who do not have job cost information available may establish a flat fee by using their annualized gross profit or markup percentages. For example, the two-year history of a design firm working on a markup percentage on cost showed the following:

	1st Year	2nd Year
Billing	$775,000	$790,000
Cost	565,000	619,000
Gross profit	**$210,000**	**$171,000**
Profit percentage on billing	27%	22%
Profit percentage on cost	37%	27%

The two-year average would be

Profit percentage on billing   24.5%

Profit percentage on cost   32%

Thus, if the design firm was requested to quote a flat fee and the client suggested a total budget of $50,000, with no other background as guidance, a tentative fee could be computed by dividing the total budget amount of $50,000 by 124.5 percent, which results in an amount of $40,160. [The formula used to arrive at 124.5 percent is 100 percent (cost) plus 24.5 percent (profit percentage on billing).] This amount could then be allocated to the cost of furnishings and services and the balance of $9,840 would be the designer's fee. Thus, an approximately $10,000 fee would at least be in keeping with the design firm's past profit goal. If, on the other hand, the designer was requested to establish a cost budget for the project and in addition charge a flat fee, then, for example, with a budget of $35,000, he or she could think in terms of a fee of $11,200 [$35,000 × 32 percent (profit percentage on cost)].

These fee computations should then be used as a base, related to the analysis of estimated time and any other factors that might affect the fee (such as excessive time spent with other professionals), and then adjusted up or down. This approach might be hit or miss at the start, but the accumulation of experiences will help the designer develop a set of guidelines by which to charge fees sufficient to reach a profit goal.

THE FLAT-FEE TRAP

In approaching the flat-fee charge, the designer should be aware of the various aspects of the flat-fee trap.

A. The more conscientious the designer is in completing a job, the more he may fall into the trap of overstepping the boundaries of the assignment upon which he based his fee. Here are problems that may arise:
1. How do you determine when the job is over?
2. How do you avoid doing just a little more to make it look really good?
3. How do you say, "I must be paid additional fees for additional services"?
4. How do you make up for time lost in revisions and corrections of mistakes that are not of your doing?
5. If the client's budget is the base for calculating your fee, how do you protect yourself when the budget amount increases after the job has begun? (You might consider adding a clause in the letter of agreement that if your client's purchases exceed the stated amount, you would be entitled to receive additional compensation based upon a percentage of the amount of purchases made in excess of the stated amount.)

B. To safeguard the flat fee, you must protect yourself from potential pitfalls by:
1. Spelling out in complete detail in the letter of agreement the services and areas covered by the fee.
2. Indicating those services that might be subject to a separate fee, such as work with architects or contractors.
3. Stating in the letter of agreement that any additional services must be authorized and paid for by the client.
4. Protecting yourself from spending excessive time by
   a. Maintaining time records.
   b. Understanding where your time goes.
   c. Setting a time goal at the beginning of the project. For example, the designer might consider a provision in the letter of agreement that limits the designer's purchasing obligations to a certain period of time, such as twelve months from the date of the letter of agreement.
5. Being aware of factors that can distort the fee, such as when the designer
   a. Absorbs the cost of adjustments, replacements, and errors.
   b. Eliminates the liability for purchases when a direct contractual relationship is set up between the client and the trade sources.

However the designer should also be aware of the variables that can have a positive effect on the use of a flat fee:

1. The flat fee is a method that encourages the designer to buy at the best possible, lowest prices because compensation is not based on a mark-up on cost.

2. The flat fee enables the designer to go outside the regular trade to sources where the differential between list and net is very small and not be concerned with how to arrive at a proper markup.

CHAPTER 12

Other Job Cost Factors in Setting Fees

In the preceding chapters we analyzed several fee and compensation methods that a design firm can use and showed that a thorough preliminary analysis of the job is essential in selecting the most advantageous method or combination of methods. However, before we leave the subject of fees, we must survey a fringe area affecting the income from each job—indirect job cost factors.

Inherent in almost every design job are certain types of costs that, while not relevant to the evaluation of the basis to be chosen for computing the fee, can bite into the designer's profit margin. Some of these hidden costs can be readily exposed if the conditions of a job are carefully thought through at the outset. Others unfortunately come to light too late and absorb a substantial slice of the profit.

Many of the potential problem areas have been outlined in the discussion of the letter of agreement in Chapter 8. If, in addition to taking enough time and trouble to analyze his fee basis, the designer also carefully examines the conditions of the job and the character of his client—viewing them under a microscope, as it were—the indirect job cost factors may become apparent to a great extent.

Typical indirect job cost factors that crop up often enough to be considered a matter of routine include the following:

1. THE INDECISIVE CLIENT

The client who cannot make up his or her mind about the design concept or about specific purchases forces the designer to spend excessive time at the drawing board revising design proposals and/or exorbitant time shopping. It is therefore essential for the designer to evaluate the client's character at the beginning of the job. In a low-budget job with a small profit, such delays can be disastrous.

Is the client the wavering type? Can he visualize design proposals? If he cannot—and very few laypeople can—is he likely to trust the designer's judgment or must he see everything? If the designer suspects that the client may hem

and haw, he can protect himself against excessive hours without compensation by including specific terms in the letter of agreement. The designer might, for example, where the fee arrangement is a flat or fixed fee, stipulate that no purchasing or specifying services will be provided after an agreed number of months.

2. CONDITIONS ENTAILING HIGH DELIVERY CHARGES

If the client's premises are on an upper floor of a highrise building and the designer purchases a piece of furniture too large or too heavy to be delivered by the elevator or stairs, who will be responsible for the hoisting charges? If it turns out that it cannot be delivered at all, who then will be responsible for the item's cost? The designer must check out the job site for conditions that will prevent easy delivery and installation, and he or she must do this *before* proceeding with orders. If pieces difficult to deliver are to be ordered in any case, the client must be notified in writing of his liability for the costs and risks entailed in the job site; and, of course, the designer must wait for the client's signed approval before proceeding.

3. JOB-SITE CONDITIONS NECESSITATING CUSTOM WORK

Physical conditions at the job site are also a frequent reason for custom work, involving such items as air-conditioning vents, radiators, unusually high or low ceilings. If the designer's preliminary review of the job has not revealed all such conditions and taken them into account, he or she may be forced to bear a costly burden.

4. CUSTOM DESIGN FOR SPECIAL ITEMS

The amount of custom design in any job depends very much on the designer's creative interest in the design challenge presented, as well as the many variables of the client, the budget, and the situation. Whether the custom design is for structural carpentry, special furniture, special fabric treatments, or other fixtures, works of art, or lighting, the point to bear in mind *in advance* is the designer will be required to spend a great deal of time at the drawing board. It is not enough to add the cost of workers' labor and materials to arrive at the base for the markup on such items. The creative cost—for the designer's own time and talent—must be accounted for in the charge for the finished piece. Too often the designer fails to take his or her own contribution into consideration.

5. COSTS CREATED BY THE DESIGNER'S OWN CUSTOM ITEMS

Expenses may arise because of the characteristics of certain items that the designer creates to the client's order, without either the client or the designer anticipating these expenses. The question then is who pays for these expenses? For example, the job called for and the client wanted a large, custom-built wall unit. The designer worked out the specifications and received a cost estimate from the cabinetmaker. Based upon this estimate, the designer quoted a price to the client that the client accepted. When the unit was finished, the cabinetmaker found that because of its size, it could not be shipped in one piece. It had to be disassembled, shipped, and reassembled on the job site. Since the cabinetmaker was not responsible for estimating the cost of installation, but only the cost of the item, he charged $500 for extra work and travel time. The designer then asked the client to reimburse him for the extra $500. The client refused, answering that he had agreed only to the original price quoted by the designer—a price that was to cover the entire cost of the item *installed*—and that he was not required to make good for the designer's mistakes. Actually the designer had made no mistake. He had designed what was wanted. His costly boner was in failing not only to consider the problems posed by the specific design but to provide for the extra costs entailed.

It has been said that anticipation is the secret of success. Whether it is the *whole* secret is highly debatable, but in interior design at least, anticipation is certainly one of the prime essentials for success.

6. COSTS BECAUSE OF AN UNREADY OR DISTANT JOB SITE

In many jobs, the erection of the building and the design of the interior proceed simultaneously. If the building falls behind schedule, the interior designer, having ordered furnishings and services, may find that the merchandise is ready for delivery before the premises are ready to receive them, with the result that the furnishings must be placed in storage—involving extra costs for warehousing and delivery. The designer should check out the possibility of such predicaments in advance and should advise the client of his or her liability for such extraordinary costs.

The location of the job may have other effects on shipping and installation costs. Many designers who operate from major market centers have learned to solve the problem of a distant job by assembling all the merchandise in a local storage warehouse until installation time and then shipping it. If this contingency can be anticipated at the inception of a job, coverage for such costs should be stipulated in the letter of agreement or confirmations of purchase proposals.

7. NEED FOR TECHNICAL OR PROFESSIONAL COLLABORATORS

Early study of the job conditions should indicate whether technical or other professional assistance will be required to properly complete the project. For example, if the job entails alterations to the building, the services of an architect or engineer may be required. If so, the client should be apprised of these needs, preferably before the letter of agreement is drawn up. Wherever possible the client should engage the services of the architect or engineer directly. If the designer is not sure at the outset of the project that technical or professional assistance will be needed, the designer should provide for such contingencies in the letter of agreement in order to protect his or her compensation.

The problem of indirect job cost factors cannot be solved by any all-inclusive formula. These factors have a way of becoming apparent only when the job is well under way. The fact remains that they do crop up and can cause unnecessary financial losses. They can be kept under control only by the alertness of the designer in spotting the danger signals before it is too late to take steps to protect himself or herself.

Clients do not like to be surprised, particularly by matters that they would not object to had they been forewarned. Designers cannot afford to be insensitive to this. Surprised clients very often lead to disgruntled clients. Disgruntled clients often lead to problems.

The Client's Budget

We have repeatedly emphasized the phrase *scope of services* in previous chapters dealing with the letter of agreement and fees and compensations, as well as in its own special chapter. The client's budget, an integral factor in the scope of services, is so important that it also requires a special chapter.

In the residential field the client's budget—the sum that he has set aside for the redesign and refurnishing of his house or apartment—is a major factor in the relationship between a designer and a client and in the satisfactory completion of a job.

It is important to understand first what is meant by the word *budget. Budget* is used here to describe the sum available to the designer to be spent on the entire job, including the designer's fee. It is not to be confused with the adjective describing a *lack of funds* that permits only a low-cost job or with a synonym for the word *inexpensive.* The budget is the sum of money, large or small, that the client expects to spend on the interior.

The budget for a proposed interior design job is approached by different clients in different ways:

1. Some clients do not want to set a predetermined figure for the budget. They ask that the designer develop a concept and complete all phases of furnishings, services, and so on, without any limitation of costs. The average designer may not see this kind of *carte blanche* or price-no-object job once in a lifetime.

2. Some potential clients request that the designer estimate the budget required to carry out a specified design concept. Such clients then react to the quoted budget amount by:

a. Fully accepting it.

b. Asking the designer to change the design concept to bring it in line with a lower or higher budget.

3. Some clients tell the designer that they have a specific sum to spend and ask him or her to develop a concept within this budget.

4. Some clients work with a designer on the basis of spreading the work out over a period of time as funds become available, doing perhaps a room or small area each time.

The designer must take the client's budget seriously because of how it affects the client's ability to pay for the designer's development of the job. It is a complete waste of time and effort to attempt to develop a design concept without knowing the budget. Since the number of possibilities for the design and decoration of an interior are limitless, it is impossible to create the right one without some preliminary idea of what the client wants—and *what he wants to spend* is a major factor in what he wants.

EFFECT OF THE BUDGET ON THE FEE BASIS

The size of the budget is of great importance to the designer in the selection of a proper fee or compensation base, because it enables the designer to estimate the direct and indirect costs of the job and the profit earned. This potential profit is related to the work involved, and once that is established, the designer can make his decision about whether to take the job or not and, if he takes it, on what fee basis.

For example, if the designer has a $50,000 budget and the job is on the retail basis, he or she can quickly calculate that the gross profit from this job should be approximately $15,000 to $17,500. *The rule of thumb for the retail basis:* The gross profit percentage applied to the selling price should be in the range of 30% to 35%. This profit should cover concept, design, and job development times.

If, on the other hand, the budget is only $5,000, the resulting profit will be only $1,200 to $1,500. Now the designer will have to analyze the time to be spent in relation to the small earning. He or she may very well come to the conclusion that

1. He cannot take the job.

2. He should require a design fee or some other payment in addition to the retail markup.

If the job calls for a flat-fee base, the budget has a direct psychological relation to the size of the fee. To illustrate: If a budget is $25,000 and the designer requests a flat fee of $5,000 for his or her work, the relationship of the fee to the total amount to be spent is more apt to be viewed by the potential client as being within reason than if the budget is $5,000 and the designer's fee is quoted at $2,000. This fee of $2,000 might be quite proper because of the work involved for the designer, and yet the client is more apt to balk at the fee because it appears to have an outlandish relationship to the total budget.

ALLOCATION OF BUDGET

The designer must recognize that when a client establishes a budget amount for his or her project, it actually consists of three elements:

1. That portion allocated to the direct cost of furnishings, services, and so forth.

2. That portion allocated for the designer's compensation.

3. That portion allocated for sales taxes and other indirect costs.

Example. Client's budget is $50,000 and the designer's compensation is 30 percent markup on cost.

Problem. How much of the $50,000 should be allocated to the cost of furnishings, services, and so on necessary for the satisfactory completion of the project and how much must be available for payment of the designer's fee?

Arithmetic. To establish the amount available for costs, divide 130 percent into $50,000, which equals $38,460. To establish the amount to be allocated for the designer's fee, multiply $38,460 by 30 percent, which equals $11,540.

$38,460 + $11,540 = $50,000

However, even this calculation is not complete if you forget that sales taxes must be paid. If we assume that the above project is in a 7 percent

sales tax area and all cost items including the designer's markup are subject to this tax, the budget amount has to be adjusted.

Arithmetic.

1. To establish the estimated sales tax amount, multiply $50,000 by 7 percent, which is $3,500.

2. The net available budget amount is now $50,000 less $3,500, or $46,500.

3. The amount to be allocated for costs is 130 percent divided into $46,500, or $35,770.

Result. Instead of having $38,460 available for costs as first indicated, there is $2,690 less to work with, or $35,770. Even the designer's fee is reduced in this example by $810 to $10,730. It should be noted that there may be other indirect costs, such as freight and delivery charges, which may also affect the base.

The above theory and calculations can be applied in the same fashion to working on the retail basis. All the designer must do is establish the average gross profit percentage as his or her markup base.

The importance of this simple arithmetic calculation should be obvious: it guides the designer in controlling the costs of the design concept. If the design costs are not established and controlled and the budget firmly followed, excessive expenditures have to come from somewhere—and it is not unusual that they come from the designer's own pocket.

OBSERVANCE OF THE CLIENT'S BUDGET

Once the designer has determined the client's budget, he or she must analyze the job requirements. The budget must be realistic in relation to the scope of services and to the furnishings the client desires. Preliminary budget estimates must be prepared (as described in the next chapter) and checked against the required budget. If this analysis discloses that, based upon the designer's concept and the client's desires, the job cannot be executed within the framework of the client's budget, then the designer is faced with the following alternatives:

1. Revise the design concept and furnishing schedule.

2. Advise the client that the particular concept must be changed unless the client will review and increase the budget.

3. If within the esthetic and quality requirements of the job, the designer cannot change the concept and the furnishing or the construction schedules and the client refuses to increase the budget, then the designer should drop the job before starting.

The designer has absolutely no right to spend one dollar more of a client's money than the client authorizes him or her to spend. Some clients, once advised that the budget might be tight, will instruct the designer to go ahead, and they will be responsible for additional funds as long as they approve each purchase. Other clients will be adamant that the budget be adhered to. The actual experience of a successful design firm is summarized here. The client purchased a very large and expensive co-op apartment. He gave the designer a budget of $60,000 and "not one dollar more." The designer recognized that the apartment could not possibly be furnished in the manner the client wanted for that amount. Rather than do a very bad job or, to be more accurate, an impossible job, the designer refused the work. It is significant that the designer who eventually did take the job wound up in a legal controversy with the client. It takes courage and wisdom to turn down a job, but when need be, do so. The worst possible thing a designer can do is proceed with a job, wishfully hoping that he can bring it home within the budget, but that if he fails, the client will come up with more money.

Failure to work within a client's budget can cause financial losses in many ways, such as the following:

1. Accounts receivable balances due from the client may be completely uncollectible or at best collectible over a long period of time.

2. The designer may have to accept the return of some furnishings and accessories. Since so much of a designer's work is custom, he or she may find it difficult or impossible to dispose of such work, so that the possibility of recouping costs is slight.

3. In order to finish the job, the designer may be forced to give the client unwarranted adjustments and allowances.

4. The designer and the client may easily become involved in costly lawsuits.

5. Damage to a designer's reputation when he becomes involved in legal controversies can be most harmful to his future.

One final but crucial point. *A designer should exercise extreme caution in stating that a particular project will not exceed a stated sum.* Not even in an off-the-cuff statement. We are emphasizing this because we know of a case that ended up in court all because a designer said, "No sweat," when questioned about keeping a budget at a specific amount. So if the client expresses concern that you might exceed the budget, remind him that you do not order anything without his written approval.

Estimation and Control of the Budget

To develop a client's budget requirements for a job or, conversely, to design a job to meet a specific budget requires not only thoughtful planning but recording the results of such planning in a methodical manner. This can be accomplished only by using proper control methods.

The control method must include all the information needed to inform the client about cost and guide the designer in developing the job:

1. Preliminary plans and layouts.

2. List of anticipated items of furnishings and services to be purchased.

3. Estimated costs to be incurred.

4. Estimated selling prices to the client.

5. Comparison of actual prices to estimated prices.

6. Final disposition of estimated items.

Exhibit A—"Designer's Work Sheet for Budget Estimate Control"—sets up the necessary control and manages the flow of required information in a routine and well-defined manner as outlined above. The best way to use this form is described below. It requires a great deal of paper work, but despite any objections you may have against paper work, the results are well worth the effort and time invested.

STEP ONE:
PRELIMINARY PLANS AND LAYOUTS

The designer should prepare preliminary floor plans and room layouts as the very first step in developing the design concept. After preparing and studying a few arrangements, the designer should select the layout he or she prefers. On the floor plan he indicates how the various pieces of furniture and accessories will be positioned in the room. Each item on the room plan is marked with a number. Duplicate pieces of furnishings, such as "a pair of commodes," bear the same number, as shown on Exhibit B as item (1). If you examine the floor plan, you will see that it is a scale drawing, complete with room size and furnishings, including the draperies (23) and chandelier (2).

STEP TWO:
"DESIGNER'S WORK SHEET"

After the floor plan has been laid out and furnishing requirements firmed up, Exhibit A is prepared. Since at this point the designer is seeking an estimate work-up, it is not necessary to complete all the information required in the column headings. Referring to the floor plan, the designer now begins to insert the information in Exhibit A as follows:

Column (1). The article of furnishing as coded on the room layout.

Column (2). Identification of the article, such as bed, table, chair.

Column (5). Indentification of the article, such as bed, table, chair.

Columns (7), (8), (9). The estimated cost and subsequent estimated billing price to the client for each item.

At this point it is important to note that items may need to be entered on the work sheet that may not appear on the floor plans, such as painting, alterations, or carpeting. The work sheet must also always reflect additional costs or services for any item on the floor plan; that is, draperies might need a line for the fabric identification and cost, a line for workshop identification and cost, and possibly a line for trimming identification and cost. Eventually this work sheet, properly prepared, enables the designer to total the estimated cost column and estimated selling price column and arrive at an estimated budget figure that adequately reflects the design concept. All this information can now be used in discussions with the client to establish the budget for a specific design concept on a sound basis, backed up by a decent working memorandum.

As the budget is discussed, changes usually have to be made on this preliminary work-up.

A

Designer's Work Sheet for Budget Estimate Control
Company Name

Client: *John Jones*
Area *Drawing Rm/Gallery*

Item No.	Quan.	Source	Description			Estimated Cost		Estimated Selling Price	Actual Cost	Actual Selling Price	Purchased	
			Mfr. #	Item	Color or Finish	Per Unit	Total				Date	Purchase Order No.
①	②	③	④	⑤	⑥	⑦	⑧	⑨	⑩	⑪	⑫	⑬

Form No. 5 (To obtain forms, see page 4.)

A-1

Designer's Work Sheet for Budget Estimate Control
Company Name

Client: *John Jones*
Area *Drawing Rm / Gallery*

Item No.	Quan.	Source	Description Mfr. #	Description Item	Description Color or Finish	Estimated Cost Per Unit	Estimated Cost Total	Estimated Selling Price	Actual Cost	Actual Selling Price	Purchased Date	Purchased Purchase Order No.
1	2	Designer – Inv.	F 2529	Consoles		450-	900-	1400-	900-	1400 -	11/10	7114
2	1	ABC Antiques		Chand	Bronze		300-	500 -	400-	666	11/11	7119
16	1	SMS Furn.	1235	Sofa (in muslin)			600-	900 -	600 -	900-	11/14	7231
16	18 yds	XYZ Fabric Co.	X 324	Fabric for sofa		9.00 yd	162-	216 -	162-	216 -	11/14	7232
16	9 yds	HS Trimming Co.	H 926	Braid for sofa		12-yd	108-	162 -	108-	162-	11/14	7233
17	1	JSC Co	FN 396P	COFFEE TABLE 18x24 glass top			360	600 -	360-	600-	11/17	7290
23		Drapery Mfg Co.		1 pair curtains			200-	250 —	300-	375-		
23	32 yds	XYZ Fabric Co.	To 2057	Curtain material white		3.00	96-	125 —	128-	212-		

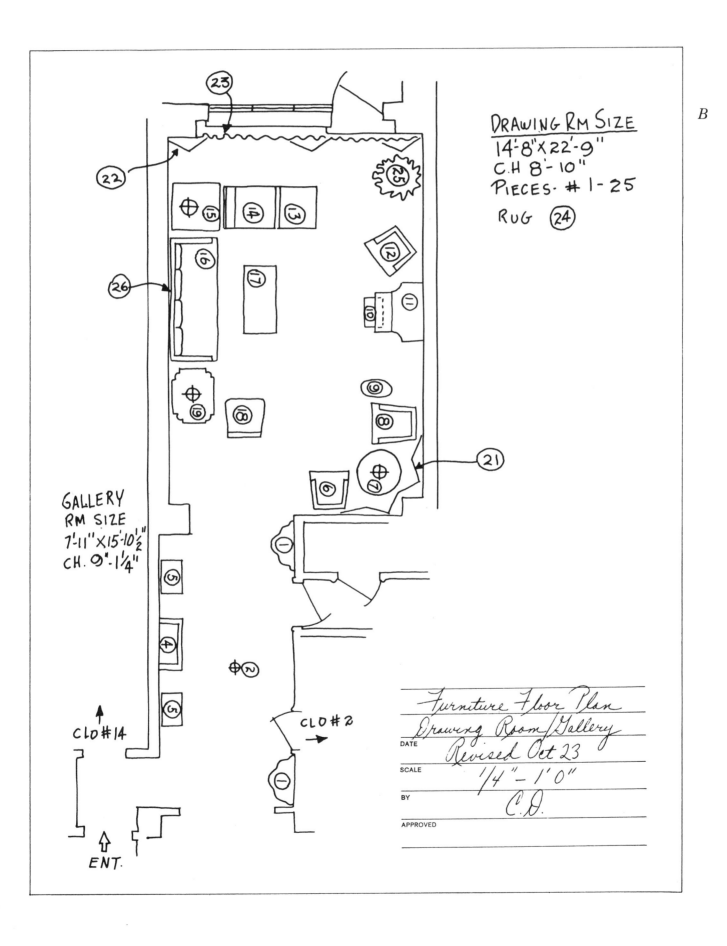

DRAWING RM SIZE
14'-8"x22'-9"
C.H 8'-10"
PIECES. # 1-25
RUG ㉔

B

GALLERY
RM SIZE
7'-11"x15'-10½"
CH. 9"-1¼"

CLO#14

ENT.

CLO#2

Furniture Floor Plan
Drawing Room/Gallery
DATE Revised Oct 23
SCALE
¼"-1'0"
BY
C.D.
APPROVED

All that is necessary for the designer to do is

1. If the estimated expenditure for a particular item of furnishing is to be changed, simply change the information in columns (7), (8), (9).

2. If a listed item is to be changed, simply draw a line through the item to be substituted and enter the new item on the next empty line.

In preparing this preliminary budget work-up, the designer may find it valuable to note the source information—columns (3), (4), and (6)—as a guide:

1. To establish the source of each item's cost.

2. To show clients a picture or sample of a specific item.

3. To prepare the final control sheet with which the actual job is controlled.

It should be evident to you that the preliminary work-up described here is simple and effective in preparing the flow of necessary information. The designer needs this information:

1. To prepare a budget estimate where the potential client requests a particular design for his or her residence without any concept of cost, and the client will not proceed with a job *until he knows where he is going from a financial standpoint*.

2. To prepare a design concept and furnishing schedule where the potential client has a definite and firm budget with which to work. This preliminary work-up enables the designer to see *how far he or she can go* with the amount allocated by the client for the project.

Once this first phase of estimated budget and design concept has been finalized, the designer will find that this budget control form will be valuable in controlling the flow of work.

If only a few changes have been made in the preliminary budget work sheets, then these can be used for the progress control of the job. If many changes have been made and if the preliminary floor plan has been extensively al-

tered, *then the designer must start with a clean work-up control program.*

Budget-estimate and work flow control is illustrated by recording on Exhibit A-1 the following selected items indicated on Exhibit B, Furniture Floor Plan.

Item 1. A pair of consoles owned as inventory by the designer. Note that the estimated costs are the same as the actual cost and selling price, since the designer owned these pieces and was certain of the prices.

Item 2. An antique chandelier is specified, and only an estimate of the amount to be spent can be indicated, since the actual accessory has to be located first. Here the actual selling price is higher than the estimate; therefore, the designer is aware that he or she is exceeding the budget. As the job progresses he or she becomes aware of what is called "overage" and "underage" of the actual sum spent as compared with the estimate.

Item 16. A sofa to be covered in selected fabric and braid. Here the control form indicates the firm that is making the sofa and that the fabric required for the covering and the braid required as trim must be selected and purchased.

Item 17. A coffee table selected from a specific manufacturer's regular line is complete, with no change in the quoted price.

Item 23. Curtains to be made by a workshop from selected fabric. Here the designer budgeted a figure in his original estimate. However, when actual specifications were drawn, the cost was higher, and again, it was necessary for the designer to be aware of how the change affects the budget. This example shows that extra care is needed in listing the items to be budgeted and purchased where the items called for require a combination of sources of completion.

At any point the designer can immediately

compare estimated budget amounts, both cost price and selling price, with the actual cost and the necessary marked-up selling price. If the information indicates potential problems with the client because of price changes and their effect on the budget or if the analysis indicates a lack of profit margin for the designer, then the time to make changes is before the purchase orders are sent out.

The last two columns of the budget estimate form indicate the status of the contemplated purchases of material and services. If columns (12) and (13) are blank, it indicates that no action has been taken. In this manner the designer is constantly informed about what has been ordered, what has not been ordered, and what further work must be done.

Variations of estimate control forms can be adapted to suit the needs and requirements of individual design firms, depending upon their size, staff, and type of clientele.

Exhibit C is helpful because it sets up a control where more than one service is to be performed on a specific item. For example, draperies are to be made of special-order fabric that has to be purchased from one source, delivered to a second source, and worked on by them according to a specific work order:

Column (1). Lists item number from plan.

Columns (2), (3). Identify the product.

Column (4). Names the drapery workshop.

Columns (5), (6), (7), (8). Indicate the fabric from which the draperies are to be made.

Thus, there is less possibility of omitting items that should be included in the budget because this form is a backup for the entries made in the budget control form (A-1).

Exhibit D is a combination of budget control and delivery control. Here it is possible to maintain control of items to be purchased in accordance with budgetary requirements by analyzing the last four columns. In addition, when merchandise and services are ordered, the de-

signer can control their status in the supplier's hands.

C

Estimate Control Form
Company Name

Residence of

Room

Plan No.	Quantity	Item and No.	Firm	Yardage	Fabric No.	Color	Firm	Finish	P. O. No.
①	②	③	④	⑤	⑥	⑦	⑧	⑨	⑩
23	1 pr.	Curtains	Drapery Mfg.	32	TO 2057	White	XYZ Fabric		

Form No. 6 (To obtain forms, see page 4.)

D

Budget Delivery Control
Company Name

Date: _____ Client: _____   Cost

Room					Date		Promised	Actual	Budget			Actual		
	Amounts		Description & Source	Expedite	Ordered	Checked	Delivery	Delivery	Wholesale		Retail	Wholesale		Retail
1														
2														
3														
4														
5														
6														
7														
8														
9														
10														
11														
12														
13														
14														
15														
16														
17														
18														
19														
20														
21														
22														

Form No. 7 (To obtain forms, see page 4.)

Purchase Orders

After the first phase of a design job has been set up—after completion of the planning, design concept, and furnishing schedules—it is time to begin ordering the necessary services and material furnishings from trade sources and workshops. If you consider the multiplicity of items and services that must be ordered, followed up at the source level, coordinated, and installed, you will realize the mistakes and costly problems that can result if a planned method of purchase control is not followed. A definite routine practice in any design firm, regardless of its size (including a one-person operation), must be that no tangible item or service should ever be ordered for a client without the use of a written purchase order.

Properly executed purchase orders are vital in connection with:

A. The design firm's relationship with trade sources, where supervision and control are needed to assure the proper completion of all orders.

B. The maintenance of an internal office procedure to correlate the buying of goods and services required for a job with the basic design program, the eventual completion of orders by sources, and the design firm's billing to the client.

Both these points will be discussed thoroughly below.

A. RELATIONSHIP WITH TRADE SOURCES

Improper ordering of merchandise by designers accounts for a major source of irritation between design firms and trade sources. Errors in designating or describing purchases are a costly expense factor that each designer must bear, since purchasing is his or her responsibility.

However, a properly prepared purchase order, complete in all details with a full description of the purchase to be made or the service to be performed, will cut down on the probability of errors. It places the responsibility for proper ex-

ecution of the order in the hands of the trade sources. This is especially important because so much that designers order are special in size, construction, finish, and so on.

The preparation of any purchase order and the information it may contain vary somewhat with the special requirements of the work done by the design firm. Samples, reproduced here, of actual purchase order forms used by two interior design organizations can be used as a guide in determining the format suitable for any given design office.

The purchase order form marked Exhibit A contains all information that would be pertinent to placing an order in a clear and concise manner:

1. Preprinted numbers. These are important for control and identification.

2. Name and address of supplier.

3. Date order has been placed.

4. "Deliver to" instruction. This is most important because deliveries can be made either to a client's premises or to other trade sources for additional work. For example, a fabric house needs to know to what workshop the fabric should be sent to be made into draperies. Deliveries may also be made to warehouses where items will be stored before installation. It is of utmost importance that a source know where to deliver an item to avoid unnecessary freight charges or loss of the merchandise.

5. "Tag." This information identifies the client for whom the purchase is being made and the purpose of the purchase. For example, the tag on fabric purchased from a fabric house and sent to a workshop to be made into living room draperies reads: *client's name/Lv. Rm. draperies*. Thus, when the workshop receives the packaged fabrics, the shipping tag immediately identifies its contents.

6. "Job number." If the firm uses a job number system, this information is needed for additional information.

Company Name
Address

Purchase Order

No. 0000

This Order Number must appear on your invoice and package

196

A

Please enter our order for goods named below:

Deliver to:

Tag For: Job No.   When Ship: Ship Via:

Quantity	Description		Price	Per	Extension

Price must not be higher than last charged.
Acknowledge order and state when you will ship.

Company Name

Rec'd   Checked   Posted   Approved by

Form No. 8 (To obtain forms, see page 4.)

7. Shipping date. With this date the supplier knows when goods should be shipped. This date depends upon the installation date or the designer's need for the merchandise.

8. Shipping instructions. This indicates a designer's preference for shipping methods or carriers to be used, depending upon such variables as cost, geography, and time requirements.

9. Specification of goods ordered, quantity, and price. This information is, of course, vital in completely identifying and describing the proposed purchase. The description should be clear and detailed, placing the burden of proper delivery on the source. It is a good practice to attach cuttings, strike-offs, samples, specifications, and so on to purchase orders for additional information.

Before you order goods and services, it may be necessary to obtain estimates from various sources in order to find the appropriate suppliers. Estimates should be obtained before issuing purchase orders for custom work and such contractors' services as carpentry, painting, or alterations.

The consistent preparation of purchase orders following the format outlined above cuts down costly errors and helps design firms maintain good rapport with trade sources. Purchase order form labeled Exhibit A-1 is another example of a form that may be developed to suit the design firm's own specific business needs.

B. INTERNAL OFFICE PROCEDURES AND THE CONTROL OF PURCHASING

The consistent use of purchase orders provides a sound basis for control of simultaneous ordering for any number of jobs in progress. The purchase order is integral to the internal procedure of a design office because:

1. It relates to the basic floor plans and furnishing schedules of each job and controls the ordering of goods as described in Chapter 14.

2. It provides a record of all outstanding orders placed with sources.

3. It is a record against which bills charged by vendors can be checked, and it identifies the merchandise charged for.

4. It serves as a control for eventual billing to the client.

Purchase orders should be prepared in triplicate at a minimum. The use of more than three copies depends on the requirements of the particular interior design organization and its procedural format. The larger the office, the more copies may be required.

PROCEDURE FOR THE SMALL DESIGN OFFICE

Three copies are prepared and used in the following manner:

1. First copy, white, for vendor.

2. Second copy, pink, for "open purchase order file."

3. Third copy, yellow, for client's folder.

Each of these is detailed below as follows.

1. White, Vendor's Copy. This is forwarded to the trade source.

2. Pink, "Open Purchase Order File" Copy. It is of utmost importance for a design firm to know at all times the status of orders that have been placed, not only for each individual job but for an overall picture of the current status of the firm's work. Therefore, a copy of every purchase order should be filed in numerical sequence in a readily accessible binder. This binder constitutes a reference which the designer frequently checks for undelivered orders. Constant review of this "open purchase order file" refreshes the designer's memory about the status of jobs and alert him or her to possible problems with regard to meeting delivery and installation dates.

The open purchase order file is kept current. As goods and services are delivered by the sources and invoices are sent to the design of-

Company Name
Address

PURCHASE ORDER

DATE _____

A-1

CLIENT _____

DEL. DATE _____

CONF. NO. _____

TO _____

SHIP TO _____

_____

_____

_____

_____

ATTN:_____ TEL. _____

_____

QUANTITY	DETAILS	UNIT	PRICE

ORDER NUMBER AND CLIENTS NAME MUST APPEAR ON INVOICE AND PACKAGE.

ALL MERCHANDISE MUST BE SHIPPED PREPAID.

IF PRICES ARE INCORRECT OR ORDER CANNOT BE FILLED EXACTLY AS ABOVE, ADVISE IMMEDIATELY.

UPON ACCEPTANCE OF THIS ORDER, VENDOR IS RESPONSIBLE FOR FAILURE TO ADHERE TO, EXECUTE, AND DELIVER IN CONFORMITY WITH ABOVE STATED SPECIFICATIONS.

_____
Company Name

Form No. 8A (To obtain forms, see page 4.)

fice, purchase orders are taken from the file and matched to the supplier's invoice. They are compared for quantity, description, and price.

In the small design office, especially the one-person organization, the purchase order that has been taken from the open file can play another role beside the one described above. This copy, after having been checked against the supplier's invoice, can be used as a master copy for billing purposes. After it is checked to make sure it is correct, it is placed in a folder marked: "to be billed to clients." When the client is to be billed, the purchase order is removed from that folder, and the billing date and invoice number are added to it. This method of billing control is simple and not too time consuming. However, because this method is based on loose sheets of paper, it could create problems if these purchase orders are ever misplaced.

3. Yellow, Client's Folder Copy. The third copy of the purchase order is placed in the client's folder or file for ready reference.

PROCEDURE IN LARGER DESIGN FIRMS
In the larger design firm the same procedure can be used, but additional copies may be required, depending upon how the information is to be routed.

A typical procedure for a larger firm can be illustrated using the purchase order form marked Exhibit B. This is a six-copy form with white, pink, yellow, and three green copies. The designer placing the order handwrites the necessary information on an interoffice "requisition for purchase order" and sends this requisition to the front office for typing. The order clerk maintains the numerical sequence since requisitions come from more than one designer.

1. White Copy. This copy goes to the vendor. Note that the white copy is a shorter form than the other copies, since the vendor's copy records only the cost price and the other copies record cost prices and the billing price to the client.

2. Pink Copy. This is returned to the designer with the original requisition for purchase order, so that the designer can check for error and maintain his or her continuing record of the ordering for each particular job.

3. Yellow Copy. This copy is sent to the bookkeeping department for entry in the "vendor's open purchase order file."

4. Green Copy. Also sent to the bookkeeping department, it is entered in the "client's open purchase order file." This is the file that controls billing to the client. The extra green copies are prepared when required for a special purpose. For example, if the item to be purchased is to be billed directly to the client, the extra copies can be sent to the client as a record of purchases made by the design office, so that he or she can use them as a check against invoices received from trade sources.

All too often the designer views his or her responsibility in placing orders with trade sources as terminating as soon as purchase orders are mailed. Unfortunately, this is not the case. Trade sources usually send back to the designer what is known as a *confirmation* or *acknowledgment*. These documents should be carefully reviewed by the designer to be certain that the trade source has correctly described not only the merchandise and prices, but payment, delivery, and other pertinent terms. For example, the trade source may detail its responsibility in the event that the product is defective. If you find, upon receipt of the confirmation or acknowledgment, a particular term is objectionable, that is the time to deal with the problem. Never should the trade source confirmation find its way into your file without first being thoroughly checked and reviewed.

B

Client _____

Room _____

Used For _____

_____

Company Name
Address

To _____

_____

_____

Attn: _____   Tel. _____

Purchase Order Number

Date _____

Due _____

Ship to _____

_____

_____

_____

Bill to _____

_____

_____

_____

Quantity	Details	Unit	Price	Unit	Charge

All merchandise must be shipped prepaid
Order number and name of client must appear on invoices
If prices are incorrect or order cannot be filled exactly as above, advise immediately

Approved by

_____

Form No. 9 (To obtain forms, see page 4.)

CHAPTER 16

Client's Inventory and Billing Control

In the natural sequence of steps in estimating the costs of a job, preparation of purchasing schedules and orders is followed by the orderly control of actual purchases and the eventual billing to the client.

Chapter 14, Estimation and Control of the Budget, described the methods by which the designer begins listing the items that should be purchased for the client and the estimated costs of each. There we showed that by using a proper form (Exhibit A), the designer could control the actual ordering of merchandise by filling information in two of the columns—the purchase order number and date.

Since it is obvious that the original budget estimate form is bound to be changed before the final selection is made, the use of this form for inventory and billing control may not work efficiently for all design firms. In fact, some firms may find that the methods and forms described in Chapter 14 are burdensome and unnecessary, because neither their clients nor their work calls for such extensive preliminary layouts.

However, every design office engaged in purchasing goods and services for clients must have a ready record of orders placed for each individual client and must at the same time provide a control that will ensure the eventual billing of such purchases to the client. There is no more important factor in running a design office than being assured that the client is being billed properly for every item purchased for his or her particular job. It is obvious that if a designer makes a purchase for a client, the designer must pay the source, and if the information about this purchase is overlooked, lost, or forgotten when it is time to charge the client, the designer loses the cost of that item plus his or her profit. How many mistakes of this type can a design organization make without being seriously affected financially?

To effectively control this phase of a design organization's operations, the following methods should be considered. Note that the forms described need not be followed blindly; they may be readily adapted to the needs, circum- stances, and office procedures of each particular design office.

EXHIBIT A: ENVELOPE FORM

The envelope form serves many purposes and is best suited to the smaller design office. It provides the designer with a constantly available, cohesive package of all correspondence, estimates, contracts, copies of purchase orders, samples, pictures, and a visible, easily prepared accounting control and cost record.

To serve as a control, the envelope form must, as a matter of routine, be handled with absolute precision. It is based completely on the theory that a purchase order is prepared for every single item or service purchased on behalf of the client. The form is printed on both sides of a standard expansion folder, and if the job is an extensive one, a separate folder should be used for each area of the installation. The column setup is as follows:

1. Date

2. Purchase order number

3. Dealer

4. Item

5. Cost

6. Freight, etc.

7. Purchase invoice received

8. Resale

9. Invoice number and date

10. Payment received and date

11. Remarks

The entries on the folder are taken from information on the prepared purchase order, and columns 1 through 5 are handled as follows:

1. The date of the purchase order.

2. The number of the purchase order.

3. The name of the vendor to whom the purchase order is addressed.

A

Client													
Address													

Date	Order Number	Dealer	Item	Cost	P.P.-Ins. Freight	Bill Rec'd	Resale	Invoice Number	Date	Payment Received	Date	Remarks
①	②	③	④	⑤	⑥	⑦	⑧	⑨		⑩		⑪

Form No. 10 (To obtain forms, see page 4.)

4. A short identifying description of the item ordered.

5. The cost of the item to the designer.

As these entries are recorded for each prepared purchase order, the designer has a continuous listing of goods ordered for the client.

As the various vendors complete their work, the designer will receive bills from the vendors indicating delivery and the amount due them. After the invoice is received and checked against the open purchase order file (as described in Chapter 15), the designer marks a red check in column 7 of the envelope form. This now indicates delivery, or completion of the specific item. At the same time any freight or delivery charges are entered in column 6 so that these costs can be picked up if they are to be charged to the client.

By continually reviewing the client's folder, the designer is constantly aware of the status of the job. For example, he knows what he has ordered for the client, whether the item has been delivered and billed to him by the vendor, and the fact that he has not invoiced the client because columns 8 and 9 have not been filled in. When the designer is ready to bill the client, he enters the price charged to the client in column 8 and the invoice number and the date of the invoice in column 9. Many designers using this system enter the selling price to the client (column 8) at the same time that they enter columns 1 through 5. This gives them immediate control and a record of the price to be charged, without having to check for this information later.

A blank space in a column indicates failure either of a source to deliver and/or of a designer to charge the client. Once entries are completed in all columns from 1 through 9, the designer is assured of having billed the client for every item he or she has ordered. To summarize, if a purchase order is written for every item or service specified for a client and if these purchase orders are systematically entered as noted here, the designer has complete control of every job.

Column 10. Payment received and date can be used by design organizations for various purposes:

1. The small design firm can use the record of the moneys received from clients as a complete accounting record. In the "resale" column (8) the folder will show the amount billed to a client. If a running total is kept of this column and compared with the running total of moneys received, the designer can quickly arrive at the accounts receivable balance.

2. Column 10 can be used as a reminder of the deposit for each item. Some design firms use this column to indicate the amount of deposit received from the client prior to the time of ordering. (For a quick review, see Chapter 9 for deposits received from clients with signed confirmations.)

3. Some design firms use this column as a guide to the placement of orders. If many items involving a good deal of money have been ordered for the client (columns 1 through 5) and very little money has been received, the designer may find it prudent to slow down a bit until the client catches up on payments (as discussed in Chapter 17).

Column 11. The "Remarks" column gives the designer space for any comments or notes. Many design firms use this to record a running total of time spent on the job. This information can be most valuable if the designer occasionally takes the time to compare the running totals in the cost column with those in the selling price column—and compare the resulting gross profit with the number of hours spent.

Using this system not only ensures control, but, if completed for each job, also provides excellent statistical information that is useful for estimating costs and profit potential of future jobs. If you total the cost column (5), at the conclusion of a job, the freight, etc., column (6), and the resale column (8) and then subtract the total costs from the total resale amount, you will immediately have the profit figure for the job. You can analyze this profit to determine whether the gross profit percentage is proper. If it is not, you should check your records to locate a possible major error somewhere along the line.

The job's profit can be compared with the number of hours spent on the job to determine the hourly or daily rate earned. This becomes an important source of guidance in:

1. Quoting for future jobs of a similar nature.

2. Reviewing the fee or compensation base if the financial return is too small.

3. Determining the effectiveness of the working methods and habits of staff members.

4. Comparing a number of various types of jobs to determine the areas in which the design office is most or least effective.

EXHIBIT B: INVENTORY SHEET
In large organizations, the envelope form may not be practical, since a flow of information and data must be channeled among the executive, bookkeeping, and production or design sections. Therefore, the envelope form has been reduced to a form called the *inventory sheet*, which can be placed in a binder (Exhibit B).

In the larger organization, some adaptation of this form and control is an absolute must. The designer or design department maintains control by using the job control procedures described in Chapter 14 and the flow of financial information is controlled by the bookkeeping department through the flow of purchase order information. If the designer routes purchase requisition forms to the bookkeeping office and the bookkeeping office actually prepares the purchase order for distribution to the trade source, control is maintained as described under the envelope form. As long as some office routine is developed so that the bookkeeping department has effective control over purchase orders, inventorying and billing clients can be effectively organized.

Some small design firms find the inventory sheet more desirable than the envelope, since the financial information can be kept separate from the contents of the envelope. That way the client's folder of samples, plans, drawings, contracts, and confirmations can be taken to a client's home for conferences or the folder can be referred to when working with contractors, but the financial records—costs, selling prices, payments, and so on—are left intact in the office and remain private.

EXHIBIT C: JOB CONTROL FORM
Exhibit C is a sophisticated job control form that is used by a large interior design firm. It shows the degree of control that is possible, depending upon the needs of a particular organization.

EXHIBIT D: COMMISSION CONTROL
A special form is required when the client (by agreement with the designer) contracts directly and purchases from trade sources with the designer's compensation based upon a percentage markup on cost. A recording and reference method is necessary not only to enable the designer to maintain control of purchases specified by him for the client's installation but to calculate the percentage fee properly and then bill the client. The column information in Exhibit D sets up control simply and efficiently:

Columns 1–5. Purchase order information submitted to the client for their purchasing department procedures.

Column 6. Receipt of vendor's acknowledgment. According to the designer's contractual arrangement with the client, the client submits copies of the vendor's acknowledgments so that the designer is aware that orders have been placed by the client and the job is progressing.

Column 7. Date and amount of all vendor's invoices received. By the same arrangement, the client submits copies of all vendor's invoices to

B

Inventory Sheet

Client

Date	Order No.	Dealer	Item	Cost	Resale	Invoice No. and Date	Payment Rec'd and Date	Remarks

Form No. 11 (To obtain forms, see page 4.)

C

Job Control

For: _____ Designer _____ Job No. _____ Page _____ of _____

Proposal ☐   Acknowledgment ☐   Special Instructions: _____ Client: _____

Est. Date: _____ Street: _____

Contract Date: _____ City & State: _____

Contract Rec'd: _____ Att'n: _____

Item No.	Supplier and Shipping Instructions	Q'ty	Supplier's Number	Description Size, Color, Finish, Etc.	Cost A/C	List/Selling Price		%	Cost		P.O. No.	Del. Date
						Each	Total		Each	Total		

Form No. 12 (To obtain forms, see page 4.)

Commission Control
Client Making Purchases

Client: Area: Fee Basis:

Date	Spec. or P.O. #	Dealer	Item	Cost	Vendor Acknowledgment Received	Vendor Invoice Approved		Commission Amount	Commission Billed to Client	
						Date	Amount		Date	Amount
①	②	③	④	⑤	⑥	⑦		⑧	⑨	

the designer for his or her review and approval. The information noted in column 7 serves a two-fold purpose. It assures the designer that

1. Purchases conform with the requirements of the design concept.

2. He or she is in control of all factors that establish the basis for computing the percentage markup fee.

Column 8. The fee dollar amount based upon information in column 7.

Column 9. The date and invoice number when the fee or commission is billed to the client.

When all entries for each line are completed the designer is assured that he will receive his percentage markup for all items specified for the job.

Billing and Collecting

The final steps in completing the business phase of an interior design installation are billing the client for all services rendered and all merchandise purchased for the job and collecting the money due. In the language of accounting the terms for this are "billing to clients" and "accounts receivable collections."

The balance of moneys due from a client for delivered goods and services is the most important barometer to watch. The client may have gone overboard, spending more money than he could afford, or he may have enthusiastically made changes with the designer beyond the scope of the original budget. As the job proceeds along various stages to completion, the designer becomes more and more deeply indebted to trade sources. If the designer does not receive payment for delivered items and blithely goes on delivering to the client, his liability to the trades increases and, if it is unchecked, can cause him serious financial distress. It is, therefore, necessary to pay attention to a billing program and carefully monitor its results as the job proceeds.

Each design organization should select a billing program suited to its office routine and should coordinate this program with its letter of agreement. Invoices should be prepared in duplicate at least. (Examples of invoice forms are included in Chapter 30, Other Working Forms; refer to Section G.) One copy is mailed to the client, and the second copy becomes part of the bookkeeping records. Many offices prepare sales invoices in triplicate: one copy for the client, one copy for bookkeeping purposes, and one copy for the client's work folder as a ready reference for the designer working on the job. All invoices should be prenumbered so that bookkeeping control can be maintained.

TIME OF BILLING
When should a client be billed? To answer this question it is necessary to examine the many pros and cons of the following billing methods:

1. Billing the client as each item is ready is probably the most time-consuming system from the viewpoint of paper work. However, it affords the following continuing control for the designer:
   a. The inventory control sheet for the client is kept current, indicating the actual status of each item.
   b. The designer is constantly aware of the amount of money due from the client. As the designer invoices the client, the accounts receivable balance increases until payment is noted, reducing this balance.
   c. If the accounts receivable balance due is not reduced but increases constantly, then, the designer should be aware of the potential danger of collection difficulties.
   d. However, at any point the designer, becoming aware of possible collection problems, can discreetly begin to hold back purchase orders and delivery of goods and services until the client brings his account up to date.
   e. As far as the client is concerned, constant billing is excellent, because it keeps him aware of what he is spending and where he is going. This type of information is invaluable if both the designer and client are aware of finances and if the client intends to proceed with the various phases of a job in accordance with his or her ability to pay.
   f. While this constant flow of billing has many advantages, its disadvantage lies in the amount of paper work entailed. Office time must be found practically every day for preparation of invoices.
2. Specific Billing Periods. Many offices set aside a specific day or days of the month (such as the first, the first and the fifteenth, or the last) as *billing day*.
   a. If billing is done, for example, on the first and the fifteenth of the month, office work can be routinized so these days are scheduled for it.

b. Twice a month may be frequent enough, if good control is maintained, to govern and follow the expenditure of funds on the client's behalf.

c. Billing once a month may allow too much of a time lapse to properly observe and safely control the client's account receivable. It can allow a potentially dangerous situation to get out of hand.

3. Alternate Methods. Some design firms do not depend on the billing methods so far described, but use one of the following systems for watching what a client owes the designer:

a. The designer requests a major portion of the estimated budget as a fund and then draws upon this fund as expenditures are made. For example, if the client is spending approximately $10,000, the designer may ask for a $5,000 deposit at the inception of the job. As the designer finds his purchases are approximating the $5,000 deposit, he will ask for more money from the client, at all times working within the funds advanced by the client. This is a most satisfactory arrangement when it is possible. However, there is resistance from clients in many geographic areas and different economic strata to this arrangement; they simply will not give designers large deposits in advance of ordering.

b. Some designers attempt to have the client pay the trade source directly, but this is often totally unsatisfactory since most sources will not sell directly to the consumer. And the ensuing confusion in the routine paper work is hardly worth the effort. If the designer feels that collection may be a problem, the solution is not to have the client pay the source directly, but for the designer to bill the client in full before the purchase is made (pro forma) and wait until the client's check clears the bank before ordering.

c. Many designers compute the total bud-

get at the beginning of the job, advising the client that the payment method is one-third of the budget as a deposit, one-third payable as the major portion of the ordering has been processed, and one-third upon delivery or installation. These terms are set forth in the letter of agreement. The designer keeps the client informed about the expenditure of the funds by sending him or her confirmations or statements. This method has its drawback in the last payment. When is a job completed or finally installed? A technically minded or rough client can hold up the final one-third balance until everything is "just right." This arrangement should be used with caution, especially if the final payment is based upon the phrase "due upon completion of the job."

CREDIT TERMS WITH CLIENTS

Unlike most entrepreneurs, the interior designer does not require a large amount of capital to start his business and, as a result, may not have sufficient funds to carry his clients' accounts for a protracted period without endangering his trade credit and standing. Therefore, it becomes necessary for client and designer to maintain a proper relationship so that credit terms set by the designer are observed by the client. The designer who is not paid promptly by his clients cannot pay his bills promptly. A designer who does not pay his bills promptly will soon find that many good sources will close their doors to him or place him on a pro forma or COD basis. In the face of these stringent trade conditions the designer cannot stay in business unless he in turn enforces stringent payment requirements upon all clients. These stringent credit terms in turn may alienate many potential clients. For example, if a designer has a poor credit standing with sources and must pay on a COD or pro forma basis, he or she must request that the client pay in full before delivery; most clients are loath to do so.

It is not written in stone that a designer must extend credit to clients. But because clients are reluctant to pay in full for merchandise before they have seen it, a conflict remains ever present. How do you resolve this dilemma? We have found the following approaches to be helpful:

1. Explain to your client that trade sources have varying credit terms. Some will sell on credit, some will not.

2. Tell your client that you will extend the same credit terms to him that are extended to you by the supplier. Thus, if the trade source sells to you on a cash-before-delivery basis (CBD), then you will sell your client such merchandise on the same basis. If the trade source extends credit to you, then you will pass along such credit terms to your client. Of course, these arrangements should be incorporated into your letter of agreement.

3. Where the client expresses substantial concern over paying for goods before actually having an opportunity to inspect them, in certain limited circumstances, you might tell your client that you will try to inspect the particular item at the trade source before delivery. Of course, it would be impossible to inspect each and every item before delivery, but where the merchandise is of significant cost and complexity, it might be worthwhile, thus giving your client some comfort in paying for such an item in full before delivery.

Therefore, a designer should determine, based upon how much capital his firm has, what credit terms he will extend to clients. Having once established these terms, he or she must enforce them as positively as possible. Basically, if the designer follows the system of demanding deposits before ordering goods, half the battle is won. The other half is to apply credit terms and make them stick, on one of the following bases:

1. Balance due upon notice of completion by trade source.

2. Balance due upon delivery to the client's premises or warehouse.

3. Balance due in ten days after invoice is issued. This will ensure that the designer has a smooth flow of funds to use in carrying on normal relations with the trade.

With very few exceptions, almost every design organization has experienced the frustration of not being able to collect promptly from clients, and many have been forced to turn the matter over to attorneys for legal action. Therefore, the problem of collection is a most troublesome one and one that cannot be swept under the carpet. It is our opinion, based upon experience, that when these conditions arise they do so because the designer:

1. Is unaware of a dangerous situation until it is too late.

2. Although aware, continues to sell to the client because he or she wants to sell as much as possible and make a large profit.

3. Has allowed the relationship to become a personal and possibly a social one.

4. Considers it beneath his or her dignity to ask a client for money.

5. Allows the client to soft soap him, flatter him, feed his ego—anything except pay him.

6. Is just too plain lazy or scared to go after his or her money in a strong and effective manner.

A substantial unpaid balance at the completion of a job not only endangers the designer's credit rating with trade sources, but gives rise to many other problems:

A. ALLOWANCES AND ADJUSTMENTS
When a client owes a designer a large balance, he may feel that he has the designer over a barrel. We have seen many situations in which the client, applying the threat of refusing to pay his or her balance, demands and secures unwarranted adjustments and allowances. (There should be no question that there are situations

where a designer is responsible for adjustments, but this is not our subject here.) A favorite gambit used by clients arises because many jobs are installed on a piecemeal basis. In such cases, as furnishings are completed and delivered, there is a certain amount of wear and tear on the items delivered early in the job, so that these are not as new or fresh looking as the last items delivered. How many times has a client said to a designer, "This table shows liquor stains," or "It's scratched" (after several months use), or "The fabric is discolored," and on and on until "I want it fixed before I settle with you." Too many designers go along with this in their quest for a "harmonious relationship with a client" and because they are afraid to lose every dollar the client owes them.

B. RETURN OF MERCHANDISE

Even when designers follow the proper procedures—collecting deposits, signed confirmations, and so forth—some clients find, after the delivery of an item which they wanted, that it does not please them. If the client owes the designer a lot of money, he or she is more likely to try to get away with a demand that it be returned: "I don't like it. I don't want it. Take it back." What is the designer to do in such a case? Actually the designer should stand on two feet and refuse to do anything about it. Often, however, for the sake of "harmony," he will take it back and place it in his own inventory. Some of these inventory items can be resold, but some may eventually end up as furnishings in the designer's own home. Sometimes the designer can properly place these items on other jobs.

C. CHANGES IN A CLIENT'S SITUATION DURING THE PROGRESS OF A JOB

If money is due to a designer for orders placed and balances are due for merchandise that has been delivered, the designer must be aware of the complications that can result from:

1. The Death of a Client during the Progress of a Job. When letters of agreement are written, responsibility is spelled out. Generally the estate or surviving spouse is responsible. If unpaid balances are not large, the settlement problems are, of course, less troublesome.

2. Divorce or Separation. In today's world, divorce and separation are not unusual, but what if one arises while the designer is in the middle of the job? If the designer has followed a sound procedure of:

a. Letter of agreement

b. Signed confirmations

c. Receipt of 50 percent deposits

d. Frequent billing and collection resulting in a minor accounts receivable balance

then his position is not too bad, except in the cancellation of orders in progress. If the designer has, however, failed to cover himself, he may find that while his clients are battling for separation from each other, he will be fighting not to be separated from his money.

3. Marriage. Conversely, a situation like the following can also develop. A designer is doing a design installation for a bachelor client. Midway in the job, after orders have been placed and some items already delivered, the bachelor decides to get married. His wife-to-be does not want his bachelor apartment or the selected furnishings. The client then tries to walk away from the job by refusing to pay his bills and refusing to accept delivery of items previously ordered. The only solution available to the designer is to sell whatever finished items he can and institute a lawsuit (based upon the letter of agreement and signed confirmations).

4. Changes in Relationship between Designer and Client during the Job. It is our opinion that as far as a designer's relationship with his clients is concerned, a clean separation should be maintained between the business and social phases of his life. Because a residential installation is based upon personal understanding and because a designer is apt to work closely with a client, it is easy for social rapport to build up among all these "nice people." But this can be extremely dangerous if the business relationship is allowed to soften and dissolve at the same time. To illustrate an actual situation: Designer and client entered into a letter of agreement for a design job, and at the beginning the designer carried out the proper procedures of confirmation, deposit, and billing. As the job proceeded, the designer and client became quite friendly. Soon the client told the designer that confirmations and deposits and all such formality were unnecessary. The designer went along with this because now they were "friends."

When the job was completed and installed, the client owed a substantial balance to the designer. At that point disagreement arose between the two friends. They ceased to be friends, and the designer found himself without a good substantial background of documentation to turn over to his attorney. As a result, he lost a substantial sum in the settlement. Whether the designer does or does not decide to become a friend of his client, he should never forget his primary obligations as a designer-businessperson.

D. LEGAL ACTION

The final step in problems of this sort is turning the matter over to an attorney for legal action. Legal actions are costly and unpleasant in most instances. However, if the designer has proceeded meticulously with the business procedures we have stated and restated, emphasized and reemphasized—with the letter of agreement, signed confirmations, deposits, and maintenance of minimum possible accounts receivable balances—he will be able to give his attorney every possible bit of ammunition to resolve the case satisfactorily. The best possible rule to follow is to do everything possible within reason to resolve a conflict with a client, but if you must take legal action, first, be prepared,

and second, don't be afraid to take the step.

Sales Tax

It is of utmost importance that the interior designer be familiar with and understand the applicability of sales taxes imposed upon the services and materials he or she supplies clients. During a job, he or she might, among other things, design the interior schemes and then select and purchase various items of furnishings and services. When the designer purchases, he provides the vendor with his resale certificate number and does not pay sales tax. The designer then becomes the *seller* of these goods and services to his or her client (the ultimate consumer) and must charge and collect the sales tax.

The burden for the proper charging of sales tax, its collection, and the remittance of the tax collected to the taxing authority is the responsibility of the seller of the goods and services. Improper handling can lead to a heavy financial penalty even though the seller is in effect a middleman, charging and collecting for the benefit of the taxing authority. Simply, if the seller fails to charge a client the proper amount of sales tax, the taxing authority will look to you, the seller, for full payment.

Areas of taxability most often misunderstood by designers fall into the following categories:

1. Designer's fees
2. Tangible personal property
3. Capital improvements
4. Delivery and freight charges
5. Renderings, sketches, and mockups
6. Out-of-state sales

Since the various states and/or local taxing authorities differ in exempting or taxing services and materials, it is incumbent upon the designer to study the sales tax laws (or obtain professional guidance) in the community in which he or she works. What may be taxable in one taxing area may not be taxable in another, and vice versa. Each state, or taxing authority, has available for the asking the rules and regulations covering sales and use tax. These rules and regulations are often difficult for the layperson to understand and apply. However,

the particular Sales Tax Bureau will respond to written requests for clarification.

The following outline is extremely *general in nature. Do not accept each point as the governing rule in your taxing area.*

1. DESIGNER'S FEES

a. Design fees—flat, hourly, or per diem—that are unrelated to specific purchases are usually exempt from sales taxes as professional personal service transactions.

b. A designer's fee when added as part of the selling price of tangible personal property is usually taxable. For example:

Sofa	$1,500
Designer's fee 30%	450
Total	**$1,950**

Taxing authorities, in general, consider the sales tax base as $1,950, because the designer's fee is part of the selling price.

c. A fee or commission charged a client based upon the cost of purchases *that a client makes from and pays directly to a vendor* is generally exempt from sales tax.

2. TANGIBLE PERSONAL PROPERTY

The definition of tangible personal property is "those items capable of being touched or having physical existence," such as sofas, chairs, tables, draperies, and distinguished from "real property," which consists of land and of all appurtenances, such as buildings and their component parts. *As a general rule all items of personal property are subject to tax.*

However, the designer must be aware of the sales tax provisions pertaining to charges for adjusting, remodeling, applying, installing, fabricating, and maintaining tangible personal property. For example, the sale of draperies to a client may take three phases:

a. Purchase of fabric.
b. Labor to make draperies.
c. Labor to install.

In most states all these items are subject to sales tax. However, in some states labor may not be.

3. CAPITAL IMPROVEMENTS

In the normal course of an interior designer's job, he or she will provide clients with products, such as floor coverings, wallpaper and painting, builtins, mirror work, carpentry, electrical work, plumbing, together with the contractor's services necessary for the installation of these products, which fall into the category of capital improvements. The imposition or exemption of the sales tax charge is based upon the general rule: "Does the installation become part of the realty or permanently affixed to the realty so that removal would cause damage to the property or the article?" This is complicated by the fact that "tangible personal property" is never exempt from sales tax. The question will arise as to whether the supplier, contractor, or designer will assume, absorb, or pass on the tax as part of their cost. In most instances sales tax exemptions apply only to the installation labor portion of the capital improvement. For example, a carpenter building a builtin unit would pay sales tax on the wood and material he purchases, and in most instances, the completed unit, falling into the category of capital improvement, would be exempt from sales tax.

The rules vary dramatically from state to state. For example:

1. In one state, mirror glass affixed to a wall is not a capital improvement. In another state mirror affixed to the building by nails, screws, glue, cement, or in some other manner is.

2. In one state "painting of new construction is part of a capital improvement, however, repainting of existing facilities is *taxable maintenance.*" In another state, painting is always considered as exempt labor to real property.

The rules governing the imposition or exemption of sales taxes on services and goods in connection with real property is probably the most difficult segment of the tax law for designers to interpret and apply, and they should be reviewed with competent counsel to avoid the liabilities that may be incurred.

4. DELIVERY AND FREIGHT CHARGES

The rules for the imposition of sales tax on delivery and freight charges vary from state to state. In some states delivery charges are fully exempt. In other states, delivery charges are exempt if the client pays the carrier. However, if the designer pays the carrier, the delivery charge then billed to the client is subject to tax.

5. RENDERINGS, SKETCHES, AND MOCKUPS

In most states, the amount charged for furnishing a client with a scale, working, or other model, rendering, and so on is taxable. It is generally held to constitute the sale of tangible personal property and is not exempt as an inconsequential element of a personal service transaction.

6. DELIVERIES MADE TO CLIENTS IN OTHER TAXING JURISDICTIONS

The designer is always responsible for deliveries made within the boundaries of his or her own state or taxing jurisdiction. However, if he sells and delivers goods and services to clients in other jurisdictions, he may now have the responsibility of collecting and remitting the sales taxes as required by them under their varying rules. The designer in this situation needs to review the rules of these out-of-state jurisdictions as they pertain to the definition of "doing business in that state." The questions and situations are manifold. Nevertheless, the designer must be informed, for otherwise the client may be charged an unnecessary tax expense and/or the designer may have the unnecessary expense of paying for taxes that he neglected to charge his client.

Sales taxes to be correctly applied must first be understood by the designer. This is a fact of good business practices that must always be understood and taken seriously.

PART 3

Special Requirements of Nonresidential Work

The Nonresidential Market

The economic impact of the professional interior designer has made itself even more dramatically apparent in the nonresidential or "contract" field than in the residential field. While the rising demand for professional interior designers in the residential field is an almost automatic reflection of growing wealth and a cultural obsession with interiors as a status symbol and facet of the good life, in the nonresidential field a rather more special phenomenon is evident—a remarkable change in the customs and attitudes of big institutions and business organizations. In many, it was once the housekeeping staff who typically decided what furnishings were needed, and it was the wholesale dealer who supplied these furnishings.

Today, however, few people in top management are blind to the crucial importance of interior design as a factor in the efficiency and success of any business operation. They realize that the problem is not to procure furniture and other objects but to make certain that their expensive physical plant accomplishes its purpose: whether that is to create an image and attract the public—as in a hotel/motel, restaurant, shop, or hospital or office building lobby—or to promote the efficiency, morale, and comfort of the working staff—as in an office—or many purposes combined.

Today's executives realize that the institutional and business environment has to work both physically and psychologically, both functionally and esthetically. The traffic patterns, furniture and its layout, lighting, interior surface, window treatments, fabrics, colors, ornamentation, signs, symbols, graphics, and works of art are inextricably related factors in one integrated whole—one total though complex design. The professional person who understands how human beings relate to all these factors, who is trained to cope with them all separately and together, and who is qualified to produce that one total design is the interior designer. This too is recognized by the business community.

Thus nonresidential work is big business involving big money. The interior designer has to adjust to many collaborators and many bosses, all of whom demand impeccable business conduct of him; on top of this he has to contend with competition.

Where the job is in a given structure—perhaps an outdated building being remodeled or adapted to a new use—or a tenant space in an all-purpose building shell—the interior designer may well be in charge of the job, working alone as space planner and designer with or without such technical consultants as electrical engineers or air-conditioning experts. Where the job consists of a new structure being built especially for the owner's operation—be it a headquarters office, hotel/motel, school, or whatever—the interior designer most often collaborates with the building architect. Ideally, the interior designer joins the collaborative team at the outset, when the plans are in discussion and the important decisions are being made—rather than when nothing more remains to be decided except the colors and fabrics. The interior designer should even have a voice in recommending esthetic *architectural* decisions, for the best way to ensure a well-functioning building is to design it from the inside out; the interiors, after all, are the reason for the building. (There are, of course, *other* imperatives in architectural decisions; for example, the size of the plot or the cost of land may dictate a tall building small in area despite the fact that a broad, low building might be less expensive to construct and operate, pleasanter for its occupants, and more efficient for its purpose.) However, it is important to remember that architectural services should be performed by licensed architects and not by interior designers unless they have the requisite licenses.

Collaboration between architect and interior designer is commonplace today, so commonplace that many architectural firms are developing their own interior design staffs to control the design and to assure the simultaneous solution of interior and building design problems. For a more detailed discussion of this subject, you might want to review Chapter 1.

Not only architectural firms, however, find it advisable to employ their own interior design staffs. All kinds of big institutions and enterprises that must continually contend with the building and maintenance of physical plants are hiring staff designers—sometimes to do all the interiors for the company's buildings and sometimes only to coordinate the work and develop programs to be carried through by independent interior designers hired for specific jobs. This is true of many hotel/motel, restaurant, and store chains, as well as many branches of government. The trend toward maintaining corporate staff designers reflects the average executive's new sophistication and knowledge about the competitive importance of expressing flair, style, and elegance in a visual image.

The enormous demand for talent triggered by this trend is tempting many interior design firms with a reputation for creative originality to explore the nonresidential field. Most of them are finding it very lucrative indeed—although their organizations may be relatively small and they may not have acquired expertise in the mass purchasing needed to deliver mass volume jobs.

Part 3—consisting of six chapters on the special problems of working in the nonresidential field—is addressed to the kind of firm just defined: the small- or medium-sized firm of independent interior designers who want to proceed smoothly and safely into nonresidential work. This does not mean that the practices recommended here are invalid for interior design departments within architectural firms or corporations, but that some of the bookkeeping procedures do not apply, since architectural and business offices have control procedures and accounting systems of their own.

There are other kinds of firms that are finding it profitable to maintain their own departments of professionally qualified interior designers. Among these are many large retail establishments—both general department stores and furniture and home furnishings stores. Such stores may have only a residential interior design department or both a residential and nonresidential design department. Another type of establishment in which large staffs of ASID and IBD members can be found is wholesale regional dealerships, sometimes specializing in office furniture and sometimes covering every sector of work. Such stores and wholesale dealerships also have their own highly organized business procedures and policies. They have discovered that the only way to assure business is to offer not merely merchandise but a complete design service package.

The derivation of the term *contract field* or *contract design* commonly used as a synonym for *nonresidential* is hard to trace, but it is generally assumed that it comes from the contracting (and subcontracting) for mass purchases of goods and services. However, all these terms are slightly inaccurate since contracting occurs often in residential work and the "nonresidential" field covers such residential installations as apartment house lobbies, hotels, hospitals, and dormitories, while many small or executive office jobs are handled like residential jobs as far as business procedures are concerned. The key question in defining residential work is whether or not the work is for an *individual* client's *personal* occupancy.

CHAPTER 20

Initial Client Contact in Nonresidential Work

The initial stage of negotiations—when the designer and potential client make contact, sound each other out on the possibility of a project, and perhaps come to terms—is even more crucial in the nonresidential than in the residential field (where the subject was covered in Chapter 6). The job can be much larger, the client's criteria more impersonal, and the situation more competitive. Because the client is usually represented by a person or group in top management and the job entails a large investment for productive or functional purposes, the designer's proposals must be clearly and minutely determined. In fact, the designer's whole approach must be far more assertive and elaborately prepared. Selling is a more important function, and communications between client and designer are often extremely formalized and detailed to assure that the designer gets a complete picture of the client's program and that the client gets a complete picture of the designer's proposed solution for that program. The competition before winning the job and the determination of fees also demand time-consuming and meticulous details.

To attract a steady flow of new clients, many of the larger interior design firms specializing in nonresidential work have over the years developed systematic publicity programs. Some of them even advertise in business papers and periodicals or in the business and real estate sections of newspapers. In any case, a publicity program is part of any large nonresidential firm's operations. Sometimes it is handled by a principal, as one of his or her many duties; sometimes it is assigned to a full-time employee with professional qualifications in journalism and public relations; or sometimes the firm retains an outside public relations representative. The relative advantages and disadvantages of each system is beyond the scope of this book, but some part of the budget of the big firm in the nonresidential field is devoted to promotion.

In most big firms, the job of selling tends to be assigned to a specific principal. Thus one member of the firm devotes the greater part of his or her time not to creative design but to communicating with potential clients, conferring with them in detail about the jobs they have pending and organizing and presenting proposals (for which the creative work will probably be done by other members of the staff). The fact that big firms have a staff allowing this kind of specialization is one of the most important advantages of bigness. In smaller firms the problem of doing both selling and creative work adequately is a never-ending dilemma. All too often the head of the firm finds, after completing a superbly performed job, that he is without the work needed to cover payroll and overhead for the next period because he did not take time out to bring in new jobs. (Architectural firms also risk the same problem.)

Conversely, many talented interior designers bewail the fact that once they achieve fame and fortune, the pressure of business keeps them out of the office on a perennial selling tour instead of at the drawing board. The solution that all firms aim for is a happy balance between a good creative and a good selling staff. The selling staff, after all, have to be professionally competent in design, since they must determine the essence of the client's program and tastes and must succeed in discussing the creative ideas as well as the planning rationale of the proposed solutions with their own colleagues.

A growing reputation makes the chore of lining up new work easier with the passing years. But this reputation must encompass not only esthetic creativity but procedural know-how. In reviewing a firm's record, business people give weight not only to the excitement and elegance of their work but to such matters as whether the jobs were completed on time and for the estimated budgets, whether the materials lasted, or whether the clients felt the installations were successful.

Notwithstanding these formidable criteria, many smaller firms are gaining ground in the field and competing successfully against the giants with a combination of free-wheeling creativity, careful business analysis of the clients' programs, and rigid discipline in their own business procedures. For the smaller firms are not without advantages of their own. They are apt to be more flexible, to offer more freedom and opportunity for the creative staff, and to carry less deadwood on the payroll.

To compete successfully in the nonresidential field, the interior designer must consider the following procedures and processes:

A. The initial approach to the client

B. Understanding the job

C. The presentation

D. Determining the fee or compensation base

E. The letter of agreement

F. Responsibility for purchases

G. Installation dates

Each of these seven points will be thoroughly discussed below.

A. THE INITIAL APPROACH TO THE CLIENT

In nonresidential work, the image projected by the firm is of signal importance in selling its services. The potential client must have no doubt that he or she will be working with a responsible organization. Fame and recommendations may lead corporate executives to the design firm, but they will almost never make a definite offer unless the firm presents a soundly conceived design solution and indicates that its business practices are sound as well. Unless a corporation has had such exceptionally successful results with one design firm that it decides to give all its work to that firm, it normally approaches two or more design firms to bid on the job. When the designer is contacted by a new client, he can take it for granted that his proposals and his organization are being compared with those of at least one competitor. His own offices will be inspected as an example of his work and as an indication of his operational solidity. The personality of the staff member

who makes the presentation is also important. So are the design proposals, of course—not only the esthetic solution for the job but the planning analysis and the cost breakdown.

Whether the first interview is in the client's headquarters or the designer's, the designer or his representative should have background material on his work—especially for projects similar to the client's, if possible—unless of course the designer is exceptionally famous and has just made the front pages with some spectacular project. Reprints of published work, brochures, photographs, and slides should be assembled for a presentation that will answer the client's questions about the firm's capabilities and experience.

During this meeting the designer must also elicit necessary information. If he has done his homework, he will have boned up on the history of the client's organization and the character and tastes of the executives with whom he will be dealing. But he must also find out enough about the prospective job to answer two crucial questions:

1. Is the job within the firm's capabilities, or is it too big, too complicated, or too unfamiliar? Will the firm be biting off more than it can chew?

2. Has he grasped the client's wishes sufficiently to work out a solution according to the client's concepts, needs, tastes, and budget?

B. UNDERSTANDING THE JOB

The initial meeting should be no more than an exchange of necessary information acquainting the client and the design firm with each other and the design firm with the general nature of the proposed job. The designer should definitely not attempt to answer any specific questions about how he might solve the design problem, what the job might cost, how much he would charge, or how he might arrive at a fee.

Just as we emphasized in the residential field, the cardinal rule to follow at this point in the negotiations is that before any solution—or even any approach to a solution—can be found, the designer must have *a thorough understanding of the scope and requirements of the job.* Without a complete grasp of the situation, neither concepts nor costs—let alone fees—can be arrived at. If, in his eagerness, the designer rushes into a guesstimate, he runs a strong risk of being dangerously wrong on every factor. The business client will respect the designer who firmly answers that he cannot quote on the job until he has had the opportunity to make a thorough study of the requirements and a meticulous estimate of the necessary time. The designer must take this position and then proceed to gather and analyze the following information:

1. THE NATURE OF THE JOB
Do you know in sufficient detail what the client wants with regard to:

a. The design concept?

b. The nature, size, and location of all the areas included?

c. The budget?

d. Whether purchasing will be done by the design firm or the client?

e. Relationships with architects or contractors?

f. Installation timing or deadline?

2. THE NATURE OF THE SERVICE EXPECTED OF THE DESIGNER
Will it include:

a. The design concept only?
b. The design concept and supplying of materials and services?
c. The space planning?
d. Work with architects and/or contractors?
e. Furnishing requirements?
   (1) Purchasing from regular trade sources?
   (2) Preparing specifications for special construction?
f. Estimated time at the drafting board?
g. Shopping time and market trips?

h. Preparation of purchase specifications?
i. Supervision of sources?
j. Supervision of work at the job site?
k. Storage requirements?
l. Supervision of installation?

For an expanded guide and checklist, together with related clauses for a letter of agreement on this subject, consult *Business Guide for Interior Designers* by Harry Siegel, C.P.A., published by the Whitney Library of Design.

3. THE CLIENT'S BUDGET
What funds are available for the job? This is one of the most essential facts for the designer to obtain at the first meeting. The designer's proposals must relate to this sum. If he does not have at least a realistic approximate figure, his design concept is just a stab in the dark. The cleverest, most original solution based upon too high or too low a figure can appear so ludicrous that it will assure that the designer will lose the job. In certain situations experience can provide a general yardstick. The designer may know, for example, that it may cost between $2,400 and $3,300 to furnish a modest motel room; but the possibility differential in the cost of a ballroom is too broad even for generalized guesswork.

In spite of this, many clients who have not taken the trouble to analyze their own requirements thoroughly will ask designers to propose what appears to them to be both a reasonable budget and a design concept within that budget. Unaware of many factors in the client's situation that the client has not divulged, the designer has an excellent chance of aiming wide of the mark and losing the job even if he works very hard at developing proposals, as the following example illustrates: Two design firms were asked to develop a concept and a budget for a showroom. No budget was specified, not even a vague span. Without clues of any kind, the first firm took an elegant approach, while the second opted for simplicity and functionalism. The difference in cost between the two was substantial, and the client, lacking the amount of money needed to realize the first design, gave the job to the second firm. Once the decision was made, however, he asked the second firm to develop the job in the elegant style proposed by the first firm—but lower costs by cutting corners in the amount of detailing and the quality of materials. Unfortunately, the first firm was victimized by this unbusinesslike and unethical procedure, and this example shows that it is not wise to compete on this kind of blind budget basis.

Some potential clients will indicate in good faith that their primary consideration is the design concept rather than costs and that the budget can be worked out with management once the design concept is accepted. This may provide a base solid enough upon which to build a concept if the general budget area is at least known and the client makes his wants very clear. In general the potential client in the nonresidential field will have a fair idea of the capital commitment he is facing before he undertakes any major changes in his plant.

4. OTHER FACTORS TO BE CONSIDERED

a. Credit standing of potential clients.
    (1) Obtain reports from credit agency.
    (2) Obtain information from bank.
b. Distance from the designer's office.
    (1) Travel and subsistence costs of staff.
    (2) Long-distance phone calls.
c. Availability of local trade sources and labor.
d. Designated working representatives of the client. (For example, in working on a country club, do you answer to the manager, a committee, the president, or the entire membership?)

The designer who approaches a new nonresidential client with concern for all such factors will be armed with sufficient information to prepare a competent presentation—one based upon the client's actual design requirements, upon his financial framework, upon the actual capabilities of the designer's organization, and upon the required compatibility between designer and client.

C. THE PRESENTATION

In the nonresidential field, the formal presentation has become standard business procedure. The designer presents the design concept, based upon the client's program and any additional research the designer has done into the conditions of the job. His illustrations may include renderings, sketches, plans, models, or any combination of these and other visual media including samples, and they will be accompanied by facts and figures analyzing the planning approach to the job, the estimated budget, the method of arriving at a fee, and the fee itself. The presentation is made to management at a conference-lecture, usually including a question-and-answer period, and then left with them for review. Some presentations are virtually competitive bids by firms that are being considered for the job, while other presentations are made by firms already chosen to do the job, with only the final design concept to be discussed by management and possibly revised at their request.

Since the development of a presentation is time consuming and costly, the designer must make two initial decisions.

1. Should the interior designer be paid for making a presentation?

2. How detailed a presentation should the design firm prepare?

Both these problems will be discussed below.

1. SHOULD THE INTERIOR DESIGNER BE PAID FOR MAKING A PRESENTATION?

Or should he cover the cost himself, including it either among his development or selling expenses for winning the job (provided he does win it) or with the firm's promotional budget? Exactly the same dilemma faces architectural firms. Practically and pragmatically, there is no hard and fast rule. The factors involved in the firm's decision are related to a similar dilemma that arises in estimating the costs of a job in order to bid for it. In fact it may involve one and the same operation, since a presentation includes both a proposed design solution and an estimate of what it will cost to realize that design solution (although it is possible to make a design concept presentation without fully estimating the costs, where the client specifies a "price-no-object job," which is hardly typical). The problem is discussed again in the following chapter, devoted to fees and compensations, in the section on speculative bidding.

Firms that answer the question in the negative—that are willing to cover the costs of preparing presentations out of their own operating or promotional budgets—rationalize the decision on the ground that without job promotion there are no jobs, no profits, no anything.

Firms that answer the question with a resounding *yes!*—firms that refuse to make a presentation (or prepare a bid for a job or a cost estimate related to a design concept for that job) unless the potential client first agrees to cover their costs—are those that are so sought after that they have more potential clients than they can serve.

But there is more to be considered than whether the firm is hungry for work or in the happy position of being able to pick and choose its jobs. It is also extremely important to differentiate between situations where the client will use the presentation as the basis for his choice of a firm to do the job (asking two or more firms to make presentations on a competitive basis) *or* where the client has chosen the design firm for his job before a fully developed design concept has been agreed upon.

The very life of the new, young firm and/or the hungry firm may depend on its getting the job. The designer may feel that he has no choice but to make a pitch, putting every ounce of energy and imagination into his effort to dazzle the potential client. If he believes in himself, his enthusiasm is certainly an asset, and many firms have won their first foothold in the field by just this kind of all-out effort in a speculative presentation.

The serious catch—there is always a catch in

a speculative procedure—is, of course, that the potential client may merely be out to do some brain picking, having already decided on a (most likely much less expensive) firm to carry the work through once the client has skimmed the cream off a few presentations. Or there may be other reasons why the design firm hasn't a chance of winning the job even though several firms have been invited to make competitive presentations or bids. Not too rarely, the executives of a corporation may make up their minds about a design firm but go through the motions of considering other competitors because the regulations or policies of the organization demand it, in which cases the unsuccessful competitors are merely being used for the purpose of an attractive report to the stockholders.

Therefore, it is important, before deciding to prepare a speculative presentation or speculative bid, to find out as much as possible about the potential client's record in its dealings with interior designers, architects, contractors, and builders. There are good and bad, honest and dishonest, difficult and easy clients, and the extreme cases often acquire widespread reputations. The worst should be avoided—no matter how hungry the designer may be. Don't assume that you can sweeten an already sour client.

In the end all costs have to be covered in one way or another. Whether or not the client pays for a presentation by a designer he does not hire, the designer has to cover the cost somehow. His only source of income is clients, and if he does not cover the cost of an unsuccessful presentation from the client he doesn't get, he must recover it from the clients he has.

The decisions involved here are not entirely in the realm of accounting, but in the much more fluid area of selling strategy and competitive personalities. One classic strategem of the hungry firm or unemployed individual is to put up a good front and play hard to get, and there is, of course, no rule of thumb that will foretell when it will and will not work. The bargaining position of both parties is affected by such imponderables as the negotiators' intelligence, character, and persistence.

Very different is the situation where the client is already committed to a particular designer. In such a case the purpose of the presentation is not to determine who will get the job but to enable the client—whether an individual or a managerial board—to review the designer's proposals and possibly suggest certain alterations. Here the question of payment for the presentation merely involves bookkeeping procedures, since the time will be covered in the designer's fee. In extremely big jobs with complex requirements, the designer may make two or more presentations before the client/management will give final approval.

The dilemma of competitive presentations and bidding can be observed very often in formal competitions, particularly architectural competitions. Architectural competitions, of course, are a time-honored procedure for awarding extremely important commissions, particularly where the government or an institution is the client. Yet even here the commission is considered a plum from every point of view. It is a known fact that when work is plentiful, the most important architectural firms will refuse to enter competitions since they are hard put to complete the work they are committed to, let alone diverting expensive staff to a project that they have only one chance in, let's say, ten, of winning. Therefore, speculative uninvited architectural competitions are used today only in situations where the sponsor specifically wants to discover an unknown talent or a young designer. Such competitions tend to be relatively unimportant, because even if the discovered talent is very real, such a designer is not likely to have the practical experience to enable him or her to estimate costs and carry through the job, so that the sponsor stands to bear further expenses in the project's specifying and structural stages.

Where sponsors want top-ranking architectural firms to compete, therefore, they conduct an *invited* competition, in which each competitor is paid a nice round fee—covering costs, overhead, and profits—simply to compete. Or the sponsor can organize a two-stage competition, in which the first stage calls only for a relatively undetailed plan and concept and the second for the full development.

Since less time and staff need be invested in the first stage, it does not cost too much to compete, so that if the sponsor chooses to invite many competitors, his costs are not astronomical. Or if the sponsor chooses not to pay entrants for their work on the first stage of the competition, good firms may not be discouraged from entering if the project is at least challenging. In such a case the big fees arise only in the competition's second stage, for which finalists are chosen by the competition's jury.

Such procedures are excellent ways of getting top-ranking firms to compete or of getting both talented unknowns as well as top-ranking firms into the picture. These methods have obvious parallels in the procedures of big corporations or institutions looking for interior designers (or architects or other related professionals) to take on their work.

The negotiations carried on by interior design firms may be complicated by the fact that negotiations with a building architect may be going on at the same time. If the architect who wins the building commission has his own interior design department, he will, of course, try to get the contract for the interiors as well. He should get it too, since the building and interior concept should be inseparable. However, this does not apply if the building architect is designing an anonymous shell or merely doing structural alterations or remodeling in a building. In any case interior design departments in architectural firms don't necessarily win the commissions for the interiors of their firms' jobs, and more and more such departments are taking on interiors for buildings being designed by other architectural firms or interiors where an architect may be incidental or totally absent—so that the negotiations are between the interior designer (or his representative) and the client (or corporate building commission).

It is a pity that client/designer negotiations are often comparable with a sparring or fencing match—or any such warlike games—but few design firms are so loaded with work that they can send a client packing when they suspect he is capable of exploiting them. The design firms can protect themselves by making dignified professional demeanor and businesslike procedures a matter of routine. Clients, like everyone else, need to be educated to the meaning and worth of professional service. The first time that a client becomes a client may set a pattern for his future attitudes to any and all design firms he deals with. The design firm needs to sell its services and get the job, but it also needs to educate the client. Where it becomes clear that a client is intractable or dishonest, then it is better not to start such a job, since it is possible to win clients and go broke.

2. HOW DETAILED A PRESENTATION SHOULD THE DESIGN FIRM PREPARE?

A design firm's presentation may range from a brief conference with a few pencil sketches and freehand floor plans, accompanied by a page or two of typed material explaining the analysis of the program and a rough approximation of cost estimates. Or it may be a complete economic and operational analysis of the client's operations, present and future, a projection of future space and traffic needs, as well as those specified by the client for its present needs, elaborate studies of the physical and psychological requirements of the staff that will occupy the client's premises, and a thoroughly developed space plan, esthetic system, and designs for custom furniture and equipment, as well as stock furniture and equipment. The visual material may include presentation boards, models, full-size mockups, color renderings, color, fabric, or other material samples, photographs, slides, floor plans, and full-scale booklets or other bound, typed, or printed material. The same common-sense strictures apply to decisions about how detailed a presentation to make as about whether to expect payment. The

strategy and warnings cited in Chapter 6, Initial Contact with Client, apply in the nonresidential field, only more so. Preparing elaborate presentations or even divulging brilliantly original ideas is a risky undertaking if the client is neither committed to the designer nor paying him or her to prepare the presentation. If the client is formally committed or paying the designer for the presentation (or bid for the job), the situation is, of course, entirely different.

The answers to both key questions about presentations lie in the character of the client, his experience as a client, and his attitude toward professional service.

D. DETERMINING THE FEE OR COMPENSATION BASE

It is not enough to prepare a design concept as a basis for discussion with potential clients. It is equally essential to think through the question of the fee or compensation base. Every client wants to know what he is going to pay for a proposed service, and business people will not accept indefinite proposals. The designer must take a stand as to what fee basis is right for the job and for his or her organization. Determination of the fee base is a complicated procedure in which the decisive factor is a full understanding of the entire scope of services to be performed, which is the subject of the next chapter. The point to be made here is that the designer must perform this analytical procedure thoroughly, so that when he negotiates with the client about the design solution, he knows exactly how the work involved is to be charged. Having arrived at a full understanding of this, he should be able to explain it to the client. And he had better be prepared to stick to his guns if the client tries to cut him down.

E. THE LETTER OF AGREEMENT

It is not necessary to have a letter of agreement completed and ready for signature at the presentation meeting. However, since it is normal and usual for financial and job conditions to be discussed to some extent at the first few meetings, the designer should by that time be fully aware of the job's conditions and able to bring the various problems into focus. Thus, when the client selects the designer and the time comes to prepare the letter of agreement, all its component parts will have been blocked out, at least roughly, in previous discussions, so that the designer will be ready to prepare the letter and the client will find no surprises in it. The subject is thoroughly discussed in Chapter 22.

F. RESPONSIBILITY FOR PURCHASES

In the residential field it is normal procedure for the designer not only to place the orders for goods and services, but to assume the financial liability of paying the suppliers. However, in the nonresidential field the extent of such purchases is so enormous that a designer had better think hard before assuming the financial liabilities involved. In an average-sized hotel job, for example, the designer may specify about a million dollars in purchases. Early in the meetings with new nonresidential clients, the designer should find out whether the clients' firm has a purchasing department of its own. If so, the standard procedure is for the designer to provide the client with purchase specifications so that the orders are placed directly by the client and any liabilities that may arise are assumed by the client. With larger clients, this procedure is especially ideal. The office procedure for the designer is covered in Chapter 30 under Exhibit B (purchase requisitions).

Where the client prefers to have the designer place orders for merchandise and services directly with trade sources, two procedures may be adopted to minimize the designer's potential financial liability.

First, the designer may prepare and submit purchase specifications to the various trade sources "as agent for" the client. Where this is done and the name of your client is fully disclosed to the trade source, it is usually your client who is liable for payment. This procedure of purchasing as agent for the client has been successfully used by many design firms. Pur-

chase order forms should be carefully reviewed with legal counsel to be certain that the manner in which the purchase specifications are prepared and placed with the trade source complies with the principles of what is known as agency law.

Second, the designer can provide in the letter of agreement protective credit terms in the purchasing arrangement provisions. For example, where feasible, the letter would require that the client pay the balance of the purchase price in full before the item is delivered and/or installed.

Wherever possible it is advisable particularly in the nonresidential field to shift the responsibility for payment of purchases onto the client where it properly belongs. However, the designer must understand that such a procedure does not abrogate the designer's responsibility in carefully preparing and selecting the various items of merchandise and services that he is specifying for the client to purchase.

Where a client's organization is too small to have a purchasing department and there is no one in the company accustomed to such tasks, so that the client prefers to have the designer's firm place the orders, it is essential that the designer first check the client's credit rating. If it is good and the purchases to be made are not astronomical, then the designer may probably proceed safely provided that he (1) demands substantial deposits against orders and (2) follows meticulously the proper procedures for routing orders as discussed in the section on purchase requisition in Chapter 15.

G. INSTALLATION DATES

The installation date for a nonresidential job is a serious commitment. From the first meeting the designer should begin to analyze the time requirements so that he can estimate a reasonable time program, and if the client has a deadline in mind, he can then express a valid opinion about it. All businesses commit themselves to a planned schedule of activities and base their operations and their contracts for future business on such schedules. Simultaneously they commit themselves to specified capital outlays. They cannot allow either their business programs or their capital to be jeopardized by a design firm's failure to meet its dates.

If the date proposed by the client is unrealistic, the designer should make that fact—and the reasons for it—clear to the client and should refuse to take the job unless the deadline is corrected. The interior designer should also be extremely wary of signing an agreement containing a penalty clause for failing to meet specified installation dates, for the designer can never completely control the flow of products and services from the innumerable sources involved. The best he can do is choose his sources carefully, selecting those that have given him prompt delivery in the past, and base his installation schedule on such experiences. The designer should also be aware of delays that may be caused by the client's own inefficiency in approving design details or purchase orders. If the client insists on a penalty clause that threatens the designer in case of late installation, the designer in turn should see to it that the client's responsibilities for prompt action on the required procedures are also clearly spelled out. All reasonable disclaimers of responsibility in case of disasters or failures of contractors or sources beyond the designer's control should be included.

CHAPTER 21

Nonresidential Fees and Compensations

In the nonresidential field the scope and variety of jobs that designers may be called upon to do and the services they may render are so unlimited that standard rules and charts for setting fees are useless. The only rational approach to the selection of a proper fee or compensation base for any job—but above all for any nonresidential job—is through a thorough analysis of *that* job.

ANALYZING THE JOB

The importance of understanding the nature of each specific job was emphasized in the previous chapter. To facilitate this analysis we outlined several checklists of information that the designer should gather. The scope of services and the client's budget are the two focal elements in the designer's study to determine which of the available fee bases (or combinations of them) will be most remunerative and appropriate for the work involved. A design firm's previous experiences can substantially affect the choice of a fee base. The accumulation and analysis of the cost records of completed jobs can be of invaluable help if the designer succeeds in relating factors and conditions in a new job to similar factors in the completed job where the financial returns are known.

The first step, then, is to estimate, on the basis of information gathered in the initial meeting or meetings with the client, how much time is likely to be needed to complete the various phases of the work. In addition, the designer should know whether purchasing will be included in the scope of the work and whether it can be used as a basis for determining compensation.

As an illustration let us take a potential job involving a new hotel under construction. A meeting with the management revealed that the designer's function consisted of the following:

1. To design, lay out, and select furnishings for

   400 typical bedrooms with two color schemes

    20 typical parlors with one color scheme

     4 executive suites with one color scheme

     8 public corridors

2. To prepare two complete color scheme books of typical layouts.

3. To prepare two complete furniture and furnishings books.

4. To prepare two typical layout books.

5. To prepare furniture layout plans.

6. To select and specify types of furniture, fabrics, paint colors, floor coverings, lighting fixtures, lamps, and accessories.

7. To consult and/or select color and materials for toilet areas.

8. To make a final inspection of the installation.

The analysis indicated that the designer would *not* be responsible for the following:

1. Placing orders for purchases (the designer would merely specify the type and management would procure on its own).

2. Assembling the items for installation.

3. Taking responsibility for actual installation.

As a result of the analysis, the design firm determined that:

1. Since it was not doing the purchasing, a markup on purchases could not be the compensation base.

2. Since the client was doing both the installation and purchasing, the *complete installation price* method could not be used either.

3. The only compensation methods left were either the flat fee or the fee based on time charges. Further conferences with the client eliminated the time-charge base, and therefore, a flat fee had to be computed. It was evolved in the following way:

Each phase of the work was analyzed to indicate which employee would be assigned to it and how many hours would be budgeted for it. A final compilation was then set up in the following schedule*:

Principal	50 hours @ $50	$ 2,500
Job captain	100 hours @ $25	$ 2,500
Draftsmen	120 hours @ $21	$ 2,520
Designer	150 hours @ $21	$ 3,150
Shopper	75 hours @ $15	$ 1,125
Clerical assistant	100 hours @ $10	$ 1,000
Total	**595 hours**	**$12,795**

The design firm checked its records of two similar jobs it had recently completed and found that they averaged approximately 500 hours, with fees about $15,000 each. Using all this information, the firm quoted a fee of $15,000 for the job, which was accepted by the client. The time work-up was based upon employee productivity costs discussed in Chapter 26.

The job might at first seem enormous and difficult to relate to other jobs, but upon analysis all that it turned out to consist of was

1. Five layouts (two for the bedrooms, one for the parlors, one for the executive suites, and one for the public corridors).

2. Selection of the furnishings.

3. Writing the specifications and instructions so that the client could proceed with ordering and installation.

The fee was realistic in terms of the requirements of the job. The analysis made by the design firm on the basis of its own past experiences proved sound, as indicated by the fact that they won the job and at its conclusion found they had earned a profit on it.

The determination of a basis for computing compensation for nonresidential work may be further complicated by the range of the firm's

*The hourly rates used in the examples in this chapter are for illustration purposes only and should not be used as actual time charge rates.

activities. The factors to be considered vary, depending upon whether the firm is doing:

1. Nonresidential work exclusively.

2. Both nonresidential and residential work.

3. Primarily residential work and only occasionally a nonresidential job.

Each of these three variations is discussed below.

1. Nonresidential Work Exclusively. The firm engaged solely in nonresidential work is usually large enough to afford a proper cost accounting system and technical business counsel to guide it accurately in preparing the data needed for the selection of a fee basis and computation of fees. In organizations of this type, the productive hours of the creative staff—designers, draftsmen, job captains, shoppers, and supervisors—are the key source producing the income to cover all general and administrative overhead.

Information on operating expenses must be in hand if these expenses are to be related to the cost of the productive hours to be billed. Normally these productive hours are billed at 3 times the payroll cost; this is the amount needed to cover operating expenses and allow a reasonable profit as well.

2. Both Nonresidential and Residential Work. The firm engaged in both residential and nonresidential work requires the same basic information as the firm engaged solely in nonresidential work in order to determine a fee basis for the nonresidential work. Therefore, the firm's accounting system should provide separate records for the residential and nonresidential work in order to build up sets of historical records reflecting the scope of the nonresidential jobs, their billing price, costs, time expenditures, and resulting profits. These records should be referred to as guidelines for establishing quotable fees for potential jobs.

3. Primarily Residential Work and Only Occasionally a Nonresidential Job. Many one-person design firms work primarily in the residential field, becoming involved in nonresidential work only at rare intervals. For such firms quoting a fee for nonresidential work poses a monumental task, since they have very little experience to refer to. Nevertheless they can use the same concepts that apply to larger firms, perhaps with some modifications. Regardless of the size of the design firm, the concepts and principles involved in the evaluation of the fee or compensation base are the same:

a. An understanding of the nature of the job.

b. A sound analysis of the scope of the job.

c. A knowledge of the client's budget requirements.

d. A clarification of other pertinent factors peculiar to that particular job which have been discussed in meetings with the client.

e. A complete understanding of employee productivity costs and time valuation for billing purposes.

SELECTING THE FEE OR COMPENSATION BASE

After the potential job has been carefully analyzed and a time study of its various phases has been completed, a schedule should be developed along the following format:

Principal	25 hours @ $35	$ 875
Job captain	50 hours @ $25	$1,250
Draftsmen	100 hours @ $21	$2,100
Shopping time	50 hours @ $15	$ 750
Supervision	40 hours @ $25	$1,000
Total		**$5,975**

In this schedule all time is charged, as usual, at 3 times its actual payroll cost. This indicates that the quotable fee or selected compensation base must bring in a minimum of $6,000. After considering all the factors in the assignment,

the designer can select from the following a fee base that will cover most situations:

1. Flat-fee basis.

2. Percentage of cost of purchases made on behalf of the client.

3. Fee for design work plus percentage markup on cost.

4. Time basis.

5. Retail basis.

6. Complete installation basis.

7. Other methods.

Each of these seven points will be discussed in detail below.

1. FLAT-FEE BASIS

Using the flat-fee basis, the design firm requests a specific sum of money to cover the entire compensation exclusive of reimbursement for specific expenses. It can be considered a proper fee basis in the following cases:

a. When the job consists of design in all its phases—planning, esthetic concept, detailing, selection of furnishings—but *not* purchasing on behalf of the client.

b. When the preliminary analysis of the job indicates that the purchasing of materials and supplies is for relatively small quantities in comparison with the time spent designing, planning, detailing, supervising, installing, and any other functions apart from purchasing.

c. When working with a client who expects to relate the fee to the value of design services rendered and not to the size of the budget. If the large budget is used for multiple quantity purchases that involve relatively little design, the client will not agree to relate the size of the fee to the dollar volume of purchases.

d. When the time needed for the job can be estimated with reasonable certainty and the job requirements are definite and controllable. Assignments with nebulous time requirements—for example, to "do a special survey and make recommendations"—are risky in connection with the flat-fee basis.

2. PERCENTAGE OF COST OF PURCHASES

In this method the designer's compensation is computed as a percentage markup on the cost of all furnishings and services he or she purchases or specifies for a client. It is used extensively and effectively.

It can be used as the *exclusive* compensation base only when the *purchasing budgets are comparatively large* in relation to the amount of time to be expended on design, supervision, installation, and other professional services. The preliminary analysis of the job will indicate whether the markup on cost will produce more or less compensation than a flat fee based on a preliminary estimate of time required.

For example, assume that the analysis projects the following factors:

a. Merchandise and services to be purchased at a cost total of $50,000.

b. The cost of estimated time required (at a billing price of 3 times the payroll cost of staff) comes to $6,000.

Then, if the percentage markup is

10 percent: the compensation will be $ 5,000

15 percent: the compensation will be $ 7,500

20 percent: the compensation will be $10,000

This computation indicates clearly that the firm can take on this job on a markup basis of 15 to 20 percent, since the amount it will have to spend to cover overhead and labor (and this applies also to the one-person firm, so that the word *designer* can be substituted for *firm* in this paragraph) will come to less than the compensation for the job, leaving a profit. If the firm cannot get better than 10 percent, however, it will not cover its overhead, so that it must come up with some other compensation basis that will produce the required income (or the

job should be turned down).

However, if the merchandise and services to be purchased at cost amount to only $20,000 and the same amount of time is required, then the percentage markup cannot be used as a proper base for compensation. It is quite simple to determine the anticipated profit on a cost-plus project, and all that is then necessary is to interpret this profit in terms of the necessary expenditures of energy, money, and time to determine if the job is profitable.

3. FEE FOR DESIGN WORK PLUS PERCENTAGE MARKUP ON COST

One excellent method of arriving at a compensation base is to combine a flat fee for the design service with a percentage markup on purchases. The method is ideal where the job entails both a sizable amount of time expended on design concept and development and a heavy purchasing schedule. For design and board time, a design fee can be computed (either as a flat fee on estimated time requirements or on a hourly basis). And as payment for the firm's shopping, writing orders and specifications, supervising, and installing, a percentage markup on all purchases can be used. The percentage markup under these conditions can range between 5 and 10 percent, depending upon the size of the purchasing budget.

This method can be used to overcome the reluctance of many clients to pay a fee based only upon a high percentage markup and to fairly reflect the two different phases of the job—designing and purchasing—in the income earned for these two phases. Again, the conditions stipulated by the client and the analysis of the job by the designer will indicate the potential effectiveness of this method.

4. TIME BASIS

Under this method the designer and the client agree to base compensation upon the actual time expended by the designer and his or her staff on the job according to predetermined hourly charge rates. The hourly charges can be stated for each individual member of the staff as a flat hourly average. It is essential that proper time records be maintained, indicating the employee, the nature of his or her work, the date, the time, and the hourly rate (as detailed in Chapter 26). Billings are given to clients with a full breakdown of the time charges.

This method results in an excellent compensation base for any design office, but it often meets with client resistance for many reasons, particularly because there is no ceiling on the final cost and clients are reluctant to accept the credibility or accuracy of time records. As far as the problem of the cost ceiling is concerned, it can be dealt with by agreeing to a *predetermined limit* on the fee—for it is possible to estimate a reasonable maximum time requirement with a *careful* analysis of the job. Such a limit protects the client against runaway time charges and thus overcomes the objections of many clients.

This method merits consideration for unusual jobs where the scope of services does not fall into the usual pattern. Consultation service is probably the best example. It is virtually impossible to estimate the amount of time that will be spent if the primary design service is to consult with architects, project managers, or the client's own design staff. (For that very reason, consultation service should not be undertaken with the predetermined time limit discussed in the previous paragraph.)

An excellent example of the application of the time-charge basis is a job to design and produce a floor of executive offices for a large corporation, developing each specific executive suite and such special areas as the executive reception, dining, and board rooms in accordance with the tastes and wishes of each individual executive or groups of executives who are to use the spaces involved and also to satisfy the demands of an executive committee. Since design-concept, market-research, and shopping time cannot be predetermined, it is agreed that the assignment can be taken only on the basis of compensation for the actual time expended.

Of course, the question of the client's trust in the design firm is the perennial nagging drawback in such situations. To avoid being challenged on the veracity of time records and on the need for using as much time as he did for whatever he did, a designer needs to conduct himself with unassailable authority and keep records with total accuracy.

5. RETAIL BASIS

The definition of the *retail basis* of establishing fees is the same in the nonresidential field as in the residential field (Chapter 10). It is the billing for furnishings and services at the equivalent of a full retail price. A design firm should definitely consider the retail basis in the following cases:

a. For small budget nonresidential jobs involving expenditures of less than $10,000. Such budgets do not generate enough profits to pay for the time and talent required on any fee basis except the retail basis.

b. For executive offices, which are similar to residential jobs in the way the designer works with the client and in the absence of multiple orders for furnishings. Such jobs are nonresidential in that the bills are paid by a corporation, but in working arrangements and profit factors they are like residential jobs, and like residential jobs they lend themselves well to the retail basis.

6. COMPLETE INSTALLATION BASIS

The complete installation basis involves setting one total fee for the complete range of services from the development of the concepts, layouts, and specifications through the purchase of all equipment to the final supervision of the installation. Preparation of this fee is similar to the process of bidding on a contract award.

If the design firm is bidding competitively for the job and the potential client does not reveal the size of the proposed budget, the firm is risking the time required to develop the concept and prepare the estimate on a bid basis and simply hoping that its concept and cost proposals will win out over all other bids. This type of bidding should be avoided by designers without ample experience in the kind of job involved. Not only is the investment in time and work too great to risk in a speculative situation, but there is also the danger that in his eagerness to win the job the designer will make a bid so unrealistically low that if accepted it will doom him to financial loss.

But there are situations when the firm may be justified in undertaking the time and money-consuming series of tasks involved in the preparation of a total estimate for a *turn-key job*, as jobs done on this basis are also called. *If* the client divulges the budget figure and clearly specifies the preferences and ideas that will guide the final selection, *if* the client's reputation and actions indicate that he is acting in good faith and not picking brains, *and if* the designer is experienced enough to make a realistic estimate, even a speculative bid may be justified. (The rationale of when to bid and when not to bid was thoroughly covered in the preceding chapter.)

The important point to stress about the fee quoted for a complete installation is that the designer is bound by it and bound also to the concept accepted by the client. The designer is not free to stray from the original outline—partly because it is in the contract, but partly also because any change in the cost basis or increases in the cost due to errors would erode anticipated profits.

For this reason the dangers of unanticipated costs and expense surprises are the key factors to consider in arriving at a markup percentage needed to produce the profit. Once the contract for installation at a specific total price is signed, the responsibility for completion of the job rests on the designer's shoulders and pocketbook.

If the design firm has had sufficient experience in the area of work involved—be it hotels, restaurants, hospital lobbies, model builders' development houses, or whatever—to project costs realistically, the turn-key or complete job

basis can be very rewarding. It requires a sound knowledge of product availability and of the kind of cooperation that can be expected of suppliers, workshops, artisans, and others whose participation is required, in addition to accuracy and meticulousness in the basic estimating of the complete job.

7. OTHER METHODS

The longer a designer works in the nonresidential field, the more adept he or she will become at selecting and applying the fee basis best suited to the needs of the client and the conditions of the job. Among other fee-setting bases that he or she may learn to apply is the per square foot charge. This fee base is not in popular use because most designers are unfamiliar with its application. However, it is adaptable to selected services when they involve large areas such as store planning, traffic flow studies, or the design study phase of large open spaces. The square foot rate varies greatly, from \$.75 to \$1.50 depending upon the service and the history of the design firm. Generally those firms using this fee method rely upon the analysis of prior job results: the ratio of square feet to gross billing, to time charges, to flat fees previously charged, and to overall job profit.

There is no substitute for analyzing the financial returns earned on completed jobs in the light of each design firm's fee requirements and the scope of services for each specific job.

CHAPTER 22

Nonresidential Letters of Agreement

We have in earlier chapters on residential projects emphasized the importance of having a letter of agreement signed by the client setting forth the respective rights and obligations of designer and client. In the nonresidential field, having such a letter of agreement is merely good conduct in the ordinary course of business.

The typical nonresidential client expects to be presented with a contract since such a client is accustomed to the exchange of written documents in business transactions. In fact, the letter of agreement is apt to be reviewed by more than one person associated with the business client; usually it will be submitted to the client's lawyer and other advisors for comment. Consequently, it must be even more carefully thought out and properly prepared. Presentation of the letter of agreement is perhaps the first time that your prospective business client will have an opportunity to pass upon your business competency, organization, and approach. An impressive beginning acts as a catalyst toward an amicable and professional relationship throughout the project, while an unimpressive beginning may lead to a relationship where the designer's credibility is constantly in doubt or, worse yet, to a quick end to the relationship.

The business client places strong emphasis upon the definition of the designer's obligations, on the time sequence of the designer's work, upon compensation procedures, and on other conditions specific to each job. These factors must be clearly defined in a letter of agreement, and the letter of agreement should be prepared and signed by the client and the designer before the job is begun.

In order to prepare such an agreement, you must obtain and organize all the facts and conditions of the job. This requires that the designer thoroughly analyze the job. The importance of this cannot be overemphasized, and you are once again urged to refer to earlier chapters on analysis of the scope of the project. There is simply no correct way to prepare a letter of agreement without such thorough analysis.

The major points that the nonresidential letter of agreement should cover fall into essentially the same categories as the points previously reviewed in Chapter 8 on residential letters of agreement, but they typically differ substantially in context. They may be summarized as follows:

1. The premises.

2. The specific areas involved.

3. The services to be performed by the designer.

4. Purchasing arrangements.

5. The sequential phases of the project.

6. The client's responsibilities for third-party services, that is, with architects, engineers, general contractors.

7. Compensation arrangements.

8. Collateral matters.

Now each of these eight points will be thoroughly discussed.

1. THE PREMISES

The specific location of the project should be identified. For example, an introductory paragraph might read: "The following will confirm our agreement pertaining to the interior design services to be performed by us with respect to the design and decoration of your offices at 1012 Garden Plaza Road."

2. THE SPECIFIC AREAS INVOLVED

The need to identify the actual physical areas involved in the project is particularly important in the nonresidential field. For example, if the project is commercial office space, the number of private and general offices should be clearly listed and their groupings indicated, if feasible. In a hotel project, for example, the description should clearly indicate the public areas involved, that is, lobby, lounge, dining room, as well as the number of guest rooms and special suites. In any kind of job where identical layouts are to be multiplied—which happens in hotel/motel, office, hospital, school, and other jobs—the number of times that any layout or scheme is to be repeated should be specified.

3. THE SERVICES TO BE PERFORMED

The various services that a designer may render in a nonresidential project are quite broad. The successful letter of agreement will endeavor to define each particular service that the designer agrees to provide. Such services might include:

a. Consultation with client's principals.

b. Preparation of surveys or other analysis of the project.

c. Preparation of preliminary layouts.

d. Preparation of preliminary budget and cost estimates for required furniture, furnishings, and equipment.

e. Preparation of drawings and other materials illustrating design concepts, color schemes, floor and wall coverings, ceiling and window treatments.

f. Preparation of plans for suggested cabinet work, closet work, and other recommended builtins.

g. Preparation of reflected ceiling plans.

h. Preparation of sample boards.

i. Specification services.

j. Preparation of maintenance manuals for furniture, furnishings, and equipment.

k. Supervisory services.

l. Consultations with various third parties, such as client's architects and general contractors.

m. Suggested graphics and uniforms.

These are just some of the many services that the designer may be called upon to provide. What is important to remember, however, is not merely to draw up an impressive list of services in order to induce the client to sign the letter of agreement, but rather to specify only those services you intend to fully render. If you are not prepared to provide a particular service, do not include it in the letter of agreement.

4. PURCHASING ARRANGEMENTS

As previously mentioned, we advise that wherever possible the client should purchase items, such as furniture, furnishings, equipment, decorative accessories, labor, and so on, directly from the concerned trade sources. Of course, such purchases will be based upon the specifications prepared by the designer for each particular project. Often these are required to be prepared in competitive bid form. While some commercial clients may prefer the designer to purchase directly and then in effect resell the goods and services to the client, most commercial clients prefer to purchase directly. Many commercial clients have their own purchasing departments transact all purchase arrangements directly with the trade sources. This procedure serves to eliminate the designer's financial obligation to the trade sources. Whatever purchasing arrangements are agreed upon by the designer and the commercial client, they should be carefully described in the letter of agreement. If the designer is not to render any purchasing services, then the letter of agreement should state that.

5. THE SEQUENTIAL PHASES OF A PROJECT

The different tasks entailed in a project should be organized into logical phases wherever possible. For example, phase I of a project might include the preliminary consultation and design concept services, and later phases might include a specification and purchasing phase, as well as a supervisory phase. The grouping of services into these logical phases readily lends itself to the timing of the designer's payments. For example, the letter of agreement might provide that a fixed fee be paid as follows:

$ _____ upon signing the agreement.

$ _____ upon delivery to you of the plans and drawings in phase I of the agreement.

$ _____ upon delivery to you of the specifications in phase II of the agreement.

$ _____ upon substantial completion of the project.

In addition, the same phases can be used to define time limits, if any, for completion of services or any additional amounts due to the designer if the project is discontinued prior to completion.

6. THE CLIENT'S RESPONSIBILITY FOR THIRD-PARTY SERVICES

Work that is not included in the designer's services but that will be necessary to properly complete the project (such as the services of architects, lighting consultants, general contractors, and so forth) should be discussed with the client. The client must know at the outset what services will be required from third parties so that the client can make arrangements directly with them. As previously stated in Chapters 5 and 8, the designer must not undertake services that are legally required to be performed by others.

7. COMPENSATION ARRANGEMENTS

The fee arrangements should be clearly described for both the compensation base and the timing of payments. If the fee will be a flat fee for the whole job, the amount should be stated. In the case of a fee basis that requires computation, the percentage, as well as the timing of the payments, should be given. There should be a clear statement of the client's obligations for reimbursement of such expenses as travel, blueprint and reproduction, long-distance telephone calls, color renderings.

8. COLLATERAL MATTERS

The agreement should also address matters that do not properly fall within any of the above categories. For example, the collateral matters section may cover such areas as:

a. The designer's rights to photograph the project and use such photographs in his or her portfolio.

b. The client's responsibility to designate a representative to act on its behalf and the designer's right to rely upon data provided by such a representative.

c. The designer's proprietary rights to the designs.

d. Termination provisions, if any.

e. The legal identity of the client and its relationship to the project (that is, owner, lessee, architect).

f. Arbitration provisions and applicable state law.

There is no one form of a letter of agreement that can be universally used in nonresidential projects. Each project must be considered on its own merits, and the professional designer is one who approaches the letter of agreement with a flexible and open mind. The nature and extent of the project with all its variable complexities should be properly addressed in a well-drawn letter of agreement.

Spending time analyzing the project, contemplating the requisite provisions to include in the agreement, and actually preparing and presenting the agreement to the client are a time-consuming activity. Nevertheless, it is one that no designer can afford to ignore.

Unfortunately, as in any business, problems do sometimes develop between designer and client. Where there is confusion and ambiguity as to the rights and obligations of the parties, resolution of these disputes is made more difficult where there is no written agreement or where the agreement is not clear and concise. Where rights and obligations are clearly detailed in a written agreement, resolution is often made that much easier.

Nonresidential Estimates and Procedures

In essence the procedures followed in making proposals, estimating, and carrying through nonresidential jobs are elaborations and extensions of the procedures for residential work outlined in earlier chapters. The necessity for going into much greater detail in itemizing proposals and in keeping control of the data throughout the progress of the job lies not only in the business client's demand for meticulous accounting, but in the sheer complexity and size of many nonresidential jobs, the greater elaboration and originality of the design concepts that are often called for, and the consequently far greater investment in drafting time required for the production of working drawings and details. The control system used is based on the procedures outlined in Chapter 28 on the job book, except that the drawings, control sheets, and samples may amount to anywhere between 10 and 30 times the number of those shown in the residential job book illustrated in that chapter.

In spite of the quantity of individual items, however, the procedures in nonresidential work can be boiled down to a logical sequence. Those that follow are systematically used by a New York firm of young and aggressive designers.

SEQUENCE OF PROCEDURES

A. INITIAL CONTACT WITH THE CLIENT
This step has been thoroughly discussed in Chapter 20.

B. PRESENTATION OF THEME AND CONCEPT
The firm's presentation consists of the following items:

1. Colored renderings.

2. Black-and-white sketches elaborating on details in the renderings.

3. Floor plans with furniture layouts.

4. Elevations.

5. Paste-up boards presenting photos and/or sketches of furniture and accessories.

6. Color-scheme boards with samples of upholstery and drapery materials, carpets, wood finishes, other surfacing materials, and paint colors.

At the presentation meeting the designer describes the concept of a solution for the client's program and requirements as they were defined by the client at the initial meeting. The designer explains the functional rationale of the solution proposed and relates exactly how the cost figures and budget requirements in the proposals were developed. It is crucial that the designer have the figures at his or her fingertips. Nothing dooms a presentation more hopelessly than an incomplete grasp of the budget so the designer must be absolutely sure of the definite figures. Guessing and blustering are not helpful in a confrontation with businesspeople.

At this stage the designer will either obtain the client's approval or be asked to revise the proposals. Where the requested revisions involve functional or budgetary factors, the designer should comply as conscientiously as possible.

C. DETAILING
After the client approves the proposals, the designer prepares sets of drawings elaborating on the following facets of the job:

1. Furniture Layout.
a.   A floor plan is drawn of every room, showing furniture in position and drawn to scale.
b.   A code number is assigned to each item and indicated on the drawing.
c.   An inventory list of all items is prepared. This step of the procedure produces:
   (1) A guide for the installation of every room.
   (2) A guide for the volume purchasing that can be easily be cross-referenced to the purchase orders.

2. Reflected Ceiling Plan.

a. Lighting layout.

b. Special ceiling treatment, if any.

c. Light fixture coding.

d. Inventory of light fixtures.

3. Paintings, Wallcovering, and Floor Covering Allocations.

a. On scaled elevations, every surface of every wall is drawn and lettered to indicate its:
   (1) Materials.
   (2) Decorative accessories: the items and their heights and locations.
   (3) Wall light fixtures: items, heights, locations.
b. Floor information: identity and position of carpeting, wood, terrazzo, and so on.

4. Shop Drawings. Shop drawings are prepared for every item of special design and custom fabrication. They are always coded to the original coding system indicated on the plan and purchasing specifications. All materials and paint colors are listed and coded to symbols on plans and elevations. These code symbols are cross-referenced to detail drawings, color code books, and purchasing instructions.

D. THE COLOR-SCHEME FOLDER

All items and a sampling of all fabrics, colors, and finishes are coded to the floor plan and trade source instructions.

E. THE PAINT FOLDER

This illustrates all paint colors, which are coded to the plans and the paint and wallcovering allocation. This procedure is followed for all rooms or, in cases of multiple installation, all scheme variations.

F. PURCHASE SHEET AND BUDGET

The budget and the purchasing sheets are prepared, preferably in book form, starting with the first coded item on the original furniture layout plan. It is of major importance that the same code number be used consistently for every item throughout the work.

The information for purchase requisitions or orders must be broken down for each manufacturer or vendor, giving all pertinent data—quantity, description, and so on with the code symbol identifying the item on the original plan.

The form of these purchase sheets depends upon the size and nature of the job. Variations in format are suggested by the illustrative material presented in previous chapters. The illustrated job book and purchasing sheets in Chapter 28 will give you a sound base for developing a system to suit the needs of each job.

PURCHASING PROCEDURES

The purchasing procedures in major nonresidential jobs such as hotels entail enormous responsibility and consequently extremely conscientious attention to detail because of the tremendous amount of material and money involved. The designer should particularly adhere to the following principles and practices:

1. Before they are issued, all purchase orders should be checked to make sure they conform with designs, specifications, colors, textures, and so forth. The designer must be fully aware of any changes initiated by clients, since they are a potential source of problems in the overall design.

2. Every purchase order should instruct vendors or manufacturers to mark the outside of all cartons and crates with the code number and the room or space for which the item is destined. The merchandise itself must be marked with a tag or band indicating the same information.

3. Acknowledgment of orders placed must be made by the supplier within a reasonable period and the following indicated:
   a. Delivery date.

   b. Delivery method and route to be used by
      the supplier.
4. Delivery dates must be constantly reviewed
   to make sure the various suppliers will deliver on schedule.
5. The receiving clerk or other agency responsible for receiving the merchandise and
   storing it until installation must:
   a. Check all goods for damages or malfunc-
      tions immediately upon delivery. If any-
      thing is wrong, a claim must be made at
      once.
   b. Make certain that all goods are properly
      marked.
   c. Arrange storage so that a proper se-
      quence can be followed during installa-
      tion.

ESTIMATES
Quite frequently during the initial contact with
a potential client, the client will request additional information about the services the designer will render and his or her concept of a
design schedule, together with a typical budget
estimate. This is often true for such jobs as a
hotel that is to be built or one that is already
under construction. In response to a request of
this nature, a design firm submitted the following (pages 119–123), which may serve as a good
guide for you.

INTERIOR DESIGN FIRM
Address
Telephone

BASE OF OPERATION:

The following outline is prepared as a guide, to illustrate the services
performed by our firm. However, the extent of services can be modified to
accommodate any job situation or requirement. Design concepts and selections
shall be presented, after thorough consultation, for your approval.

DESIGN SERVICES:

1. Prepare for your approval designs, layouts, furniture and furnishings for
    Hotel Rooms, Public Corridors and Elevator Foyers.

2. Prepare for your approval concept renderings of areas under consideration.

3. Specifically, we will select furniture, fabrics, i.e. upholstery, drapery,
    bedspreads, paint colors and/or wallcoverings, floor coverings, lighting
    fixtures, lamps and decorative accessories for your approval.

4. Prepare for quantity take-off and installation, individual floor furniture
    plans, indicating by room numbers, a count schedule, coded color schemes,
    and paint/wallcovering allocation.

5. Prepare for purchasing and installation typical room and suite floor plans,
    color schemes, and picture installation elevations. This information is
    presented in bound book form.

6. Prepare for purchasing and job record, furniture and furnishings books,
    pictorially illustrating those items, including specifications, disposition,
    upholstery and finish. This information is presented in bound book form.

7. We will inspect all furniture and furnishings either in production, phototypes
    or shop drawings as required.

8. We will coordinate with building architect regarding material and color
    selections for toilets, dressing areas, corridors and elevator lobbies.

9. We shall periodically inspect installation as required.

REMUNERATION

1. Will be a design fee, which is based on amount of time to perform the
    required services.

2. Out-of-pocket expenses directly associated with the execution of this
    commission, shall be reimbursed.

3. Concept renderings shall be billed to you at our cost.

SECTION 1

PAGE 2

PURCHASING

1. We will prepare purchase orders on your stationery, which will be returned to you for your review, authorization, deposit (if necessary) and issuance to vendor.

2. Each purchase order prepared by this office shall contain in addition to quantity, specifications, etc., containing marking instructions to facilitate installation.

3. For the preparation of purchase orders we shall be remunerated on a fee basis.

CLIENT RESPONSIBILITY

1. Selection of a receiving agent who will receive, inspect, store and install furnishings.

2. Coordinator who will act as liaison and prepare site installation, schedule and coordinate with receiving agent.

3. Payment of all vendors bills.

4. Payment of receiving agent, storage and installation costs.

If our firm's services are engaged, a letter of agreement setting forth our respective obligations will be drawn up.

SCHEDULE 2

PAGE 1

Prepared by
Interior Design Firm

PROPOSED DESIGN SCHEDULE

| FLOORS | DESIGN PERIODS | COLOR SCHEDULES | | ROOM TYPE | | | TOTAL ROOMS |
	-	L.R.	B.R.	LANAI	L.R.	B.R.	-
Lanai	1	1	-	9	0	0	9
2nd Floor	1	1	2	0	4	29	33 (2 alcoves)
3rd Floor	Same as 2nd Floor	Same as 2nd Floor	Same as 2nd Floor	0	2	31	33
4th Floor	1	1	2	0	2	31	33
5th Floor	Same as 4th Floor	Same as 4th Floor	Same as 4th Floor	0	2	31	33
6th Floor	1	1	2	0	2	31	33
7th Floor	Same as 6th Floor	Same as 6th Floor	Same as 6th Floor	0	2	31	33
8th Floor Upper/Lower							
Town House Suites	Same as 2nd Floor	Same as 2nd Floor	Same as 2nd Floor	0	14	14	28
Royal Suite	1	1	2	0	1	2	3
Deluxe Suites	Same as 4th Floor	Same as 4th Floor	Same as 4th Floor	0	6	12	18
Special Suites	Same as 6th Floor	2	3	0	2	3	5
Total Design Periods	5						
Total Color Schemes		8	11				
Total Room Types				9	37	215	
Total Rooms							261

SCHEDULE 3

PAGE 1

Prepared by
Interior design firm

PROPOSED FURNISHINGS BUDGET FOR
TYPICAL LIVING ROOM (TOWN HOUSE SUITES)

Carpet	50 yd	$15.00	$750.00	
Padding	50 yd	1.80	90.00	
Labor	50 yd	2.50	125.00	
		Carpet Total		$ 965.00
One 60" sofa				500.00
Fabric for above 12 yd		$ 12.00		144.00
Three lounge chairs		250.00		750.00
Fabric for above 18 yd		12.00		216.00
Two end tables		120.00		240.00
One occasional table				100.00
One credenza				450.00
One dining/game table				250.00
Four side chairs		125.00		500.00
Fabric for above 4 yd		12.00		48.00
One mirror				120.00
Five pictures				170.00
One table lamp				50.00
Three lamps		30.00		90.00
One pair of draperies, 10 widths wide				
milium lined, labor, hardware, and installation				180.00
Fabric for above 40 yd				220.00
One pair of undercurtains 11 widths wide				
labor, hardware, and installation				120.00
Fabric for above 44 yd		3.00		132.00
One soft valance, milium lined, labor, hardware,				
and installation				160.00
Fabric for above 18 yd		9.00		162.00
				$5,567.00

Note: The above does not include
Shipping charges
Travel expenses

SCHEDULE 4

PAGE 1

Prepared by
Interior design firm

PROPOSED FURNITURE BUDGET FOR
TYPICAL BEDROOM

Carpet 42 yd	$10.00		$420.00	
Padding 42 yd	1.80		76.00	
Labor 42 yd	2.25		94.00	
		Carpet Total		$ 590.00
Two 39" headboards			80.00	160.00
Two carriers			16.00	32.00
Two 39" x 80" box spring & mattress			75.00	150.00
One night table				120.00
Two lounge chairs			250.00	500.00
Fabric for above 12 yd			12.00	144.00
One 48" desk				220.00
One desk chair with arms				125.00
Fabric for above 1 yd				12.00
One table lamp				50.00
One night table lamp				30.00
One desk lamp				30.00
Six pictures				150.00
Two bedspreads:				
Labor to make spread and dust ruffle			40.00	80.00
Fabric for above 26 yd			6.00	156.00
One pair of draperies, 10 widths wide				
milium lined, labor, hardware, and installation				180.00
Fabric for above 40 yd			6.00	240.00
One pair of undercurtains, 11 widths wide				
labor, hardware, and installation				120.00
Fabric for above 40 yd			3.00	120.00
One soft valance, milium lined,				
labor, hardware, and installation				160.00
Fabric for above 18 yd			9.00	162.00
				$3,531.00

Note: The above does not include:
            Builtin chest
            Shipping charges
            Travel expenses

PART 4

Special Factors, Forms, and Techniques

The Interior Designer as a Product Designer

Interior designers often find themselves engaged in product design without even realizing that they have changed hats. While the configuration of a specific room necessitates using a particular size and type of cabinet in order to complete the designer's scheme, such a cabinet is not available in the regular line of any resource. The designer prepares a scale drawing of what is required and works with his or her custom cabinetmaker to select materials, hardware, and finish for the production of this special order item, which is to be used only in the job in question.

A bank president desires something special in the decor of his new central branch. The designer works the bank's corporate motif into a special design for an area rug or wallhanging and works with a custom carpet manufacturer or tapestrymaker to produce this special item.

To satisfy the client's desire for central control over all elements of a contemplated media room, the designer creates a special control table that meets the need without adversely affecting the planned decor of the room. The table is custom built to the designer's specifications.

These examples illustrate several of the myriad instances where designers are involved in the creation of a product; in most such instances, the designer considers this work simply a part of the interior design job. In other instances, a particular designer becomes known for his or her use of a specific style of furniture, be it upholstery or case goods. In order to ensure continuity of his or her "look," the designer will work with an upholsterer or cabinetmaker to create a line of items that are to be produced on a custom basis solely for the designer's use in subsequent jobs. In still other instances where the volume of business warrants, interior design firms have developed their own fabric lines that are custom produced solely for the use of that design firm.

Designers from time to time will participate in contests for the design of an area rug, fabric, a new style of recliner chair, and so on, with such competition clearly requiring product design. Such activities have often led designers to undertake product design either as an adjunct to their interior design work or as a wholly separate business with production usually intended for sale to other interior designers.

Some designers will either sporadically or regularly design a line of fabrics or wallpapers, or a collection of area rugs or a group of furniture for a third party, who will then produce and market the items to other designers. Others have been instrumental in establishing resource firms that regularly market on a national basis such products as reproduction furniture, upholstery, fabrics, and wallpaper. The prime customers of such firms are other interior designers.

In recent years, designers have expanded such activities beyond the interior design market and are more and more frequently involved in the design of products manufactured for sale to the public at retail. Some have even completely changed hats and now confine their activities to designing products for the mass manufacturer.

THREE COMPONENTS OF A PRODUCT DESIGN PROGRAM

All this participation in product design makes it necessary for today's interior design practitioner to be at least generally familiar with the business opportunities and responsibilities inherent in this type of work. Such involvement requires that the designer make decisions on three separate elements that pertain to any product design program.

1. The prime element is the type of product or products involved. Product possibilities include not only the decorative merchandise with which the designer is traditionally familiar—fabrics, wallpaper, rugs, furniture, lamps, and accessories—but the multitude of other items marketed directly to the consumer through retail outlets. The latter comprise all the same types of products as are available in the decorative market, but extend as well to such domestic

items as sheets, pillowcases, blankets, comforters, bedspreads, and other bed ensembles; to bathroom items such as towels, bath rugs, shower curtains, and bath accessories; to such table linen items as tablecloths, tablemats, napkins, and the like; to kitchen items such as towels, mitts, cutlery, pots and pans, and accessories; and to such table-top items as flatware, fine china, earthenware, glasses, barware, giftware, and accessories; and yes, today, even to home fragrances.

2. The second key element is the intended market. Will the product be marketed through a resource firm on an individual, more-or-less custom basis to decorative market buyers? Will the product be marketed through so-called contract resource firms to commercial buyers using the services of architects, purchasing agents, or other specifiers? Will the product be marketed directly to the consumer through department stores and other quality retail establishments? Will the product be marketed to that segment of the public that buys at chain stores?

3. The third element pertains to the extent and purpose of the program. Will it involve a single product such as an area rug to be added to the line of either a decorative or a mass market manufacturer? Will it involve a product collection with several distinct but coordinated designs incorporated into a number of products such as sheets, towels, and bedspreads intended to be produced by a single manufacturer and introduced at a specific wholesale market? Will it involve a continuous program for a particular manufacturer such as the design of a collection of furniture items with additional models being added at semiannual or annual intervals over a number of years? Will it involve a large number of coordinated but different products such as domestics, table linens, and furniture to be produced by a number of separate manufacturers but marketed through department stores or so-called designer-concept shops in department stores?

The determination of the three elements will not only fix the scope of the product design program, but will largely establish whether or not the products will be marketed under the designer's name, since this question is essentially answered by the quality of product and intended market.

Apart from those instances where a designer establishes his own resource firm or confines his product work to the occasional special design required for a client's interior, getting started in the product field is not easy, either for an interior designer or, for that matter, any other type of designer. Many resource firms and retail product manufacturers are reluctant to use independent designers to create their merchandise lines because of attendant cost factors, as well as inhouse personnel problems that may at times arise. Nevertheless, following the lead of fashion, name design is becoming more important in the world of interior products.

In consequence, leading designers whose reputations and standing in the interior design field are well established or whose work is regularly featured in the interior design or general press are today considered serious candidates to develop new lines for product manufacturers, especially if the designer has become known for a particular look that is compatible with the particular product. Sometimes designers have taken the initiative by directly approaching product manufacturers or by hiring agents to search out ways by which the designer can create a line of products for a particular manufacturer or group of manufacturers. Useful in all this is the ability to demonstrate prior comparable work.

For example, a designer known for developing a line of geometric-patterned decorative fabrics is likely to have a substantial advantage when a sheet mill is considering producing a collection of domestics with a geometric motif. At times it is equally useful to present a portfolio of either sketches or complete designs for the specific product category or to demonstrate to the manufacturer's satisfaction that the designer or his or her staff is capable of producing the required designs painted in repeat, the scale shop drawings, models, or other materials that will significantly reduce the manufacturer's inhouse requirements in creating a new product line.

However, as in the fashion field, fame is the name of the game, and the well-known name will always receive consideration. Since success breeds success, the designer whose sheets are being featured in department stores throughout the country is likely to be approached in ensuing seasons by manufacturers of other types of products.

KEY ELEMENTS IN THE DESIGNER-MANUFACTURER ARRANGEMENT

Assuming a manufacturer is interested, what are the key elements of the arrangement? The design could be sold either for a fixed price or for an amount calculated under a sales royalty, but there are certain drawbacks to either sales procedure. For example, unless prohibited by express agreement, all proprietary rights to the design pass to the manufacturer, who is entitled to use or authorize others to use the design for wholly different products without the designer receiving any additional compensation or, for that matter, design credit. Again, unless governed by express agreement, it would be difficult for the designer to exercise quality control over a product whose design is now owned by a manufacturer. This could be particularly vexing where the product is advertised and marketed under the designer's name.

On the other hand, if it is possible to apply for either a design patent or a mechanical patent for the particular design, then the drawbacks of the sale method could well be outweighed by the favorable capital gains tax treatment afforded the sales price, whether that is a fixed or a royalty amount determined by the extent of sales. From the manufacturer's point of view, the sales method has equivalent drawbacks, particularly where its purpose is to ensure an ongoing relationship with the designer. Al-

though these problems can be overcome by an appropriate agreement, it has become almost universal in arrangements between name designers and manufacturing firms for designs to be licensed rather than sold to the manufacturer.

The key distinction is the fact that a license reserves to the designer the proprietary rights in the design and permits the manufacturer only the right to use them for specific purposes and pursuant to specific arrangements and controls spelled out in the license agreement.

While it is beyond the scope of this chapter to explore in detail the intricacies of a properly prepared product design license agreement or product design sales agreement (for which the designer should seek legal advice), it is pertinent to touch on the various elements that should be covered in such an agreement.

DESIGN SERVICES

An arrangement could be confined to the use of existing designs prepared to secure the arrangement or for other purposes, or it could require that wholly new designs be created to fit the specific product category or manufacturer's requirements.

Presentation of design work will, depending upon the nature of the product, require black and white or color sketches, scale drawings, artwork painted in repeat, shop drawings, airbrush artwork, or models. Wallpapers, fabrics, and the multitude of other products incorporating the use of fabrics will generally require any number of different colorways per individual design.

Production processes may require the direct involvement of the designer in approval of strikeoffs or other initial samples or in the preparation of product mockups or prototypes. In many instances the designer must work closely with the manufacturer's personnel at the production site to ensure that production procedures will result in the manufacture of production merchandise equivalent to approved samples.

Promotion and publicity are often the keys to successfully launching a new product and can well involve the designer personally in market openings, retail store sales tours, and meetings with manufacturer's sales personnel.

The extent to which the designer and his or her staff are responsible for each type of service should be carefully spelled out in the agreement, from the viewpoint not only of limiting the designer's responsibility, where applicable, but of enhancing the designer's right to participate directly in areas that might otherwise be left to the tender mercies of the manufacturer's inhouse design staff. Equally important is the need to set forth timing requirements, since in the product world there are meaningful deadlines that must be met.

COMPENSATION

The work can be done for a fixed fee calculated either on the basis of prior experience or on the basis of what the designer believes his or her creativity is worth or, as most likely, determined by direct negotiation with the manufacturer. Fixed fee arrangements are more common where designs are sold.

In license arrangements, compensation is generally based on the payment of royalties, but where the designer is nationally known or otherwise has standing in the field, it is not unusual for the royalty arrangement to be enhanced by either the addition of a fixed fee or a guarantee that a minimum amount will be paid over the course of the contract. In some instances the additional fixed fee or minimum payment is over and above royalty payments otherwise generated, but it is more likely for such fixed fee or guaranteed minimum to be credited against royalties.

Payment methods are as varied as in any other form of commercial contract. The only common denominator is that they are generally spread over either the life of the contract or the sales life of the product.

ROYALTY BASIS

Although hardly universal, it is general practice to pay royalties on the basis of a percentage of the product's "net sales" for as long as the product continues to be marketed. Royalty percentages can vary from as little as 1 percent (generally mass market items sold without use of the designer's name) to 12 percent (generally items with high unit cost and moderate aggregate volume) to as much as 15 percent (generally special items sold in the decorative market). There is no hard and fast rule to any of this, and the percentage chosen is likely to depend upon direct negotiation with the particular manufacturer. Here the manufacturer's prior experience, if any, with design royalty arrangements is likely to be a significant factor.

Net sales are generally determined on a commercial basis and often will exclude merchandise sold as seconds or closed out because the item either has not been marketed successfully or has reached the end of its marketable life span.

Another method for determining royalties is to apply the agreed-upon percentage to the unit cost, which is either the factory cost or, in the case of products manufactured abroad, the first import cost. These methods are less favorable to the designer since they are predicated on a base lower than net sales. Still another method is to fix the royalty on the basis of a dollar amount per sold unit; for example, $.20 per linear yard of the total number of yards of fabric sold or $100 per table sold or per area rug sold.

REPORTS AND RECORDS

Whatever the royalty method, the arrangement should provide for appropriate reports to be submitted at regular intervals, either monthly or quarterly, pertaining to production and sales. Depending upon the royalty method, each report should set forth all data required to determine the royalty payable to the designer and should be certified as correct by an appropriate official of the manufacturer. Beside such certification, the designer should retain the right to have his or her accounting representative examine the manufacturer's books and records from time to time to confirm the report data submitted by the manufacturer. This right, of course, should be exercised only when warranted by relevant circumstances.

CONTROLS

The key here is control over the quality of the product, particularly where it is marketed under the designer's name. This is usually accomplished by requiring the designer's reasonable approval of strikeoffs, samples, or prototypes. However, this is really not sufficient, and the designer should insist upon the right to prevent the sale of merchandise under his or her name if production merchandise does not reasonably conform to the approved sample.

You will note the use of the word "reasonable" in the preceding paragraph. It must be kept in mind that there are different levels of quality and that the designer cannot expect merchandise produced for sale through chain stores at a price appropriate to such a market to have the quality equivalent to merchandise intended for sale through decorative resources.

Equally important to control of product quality is control of the use of the designer's name. In the usual arrangement, the name will appear not only on the product's label but in packaging, advertisements, and public relations materials. Since manufacturers at times are more interested in enhancing their own brand name, it is important to carefully define in the arrangement the manner in which the designer's name will be used and whether it is to be used alone or in conjunction with the manufacturer's brand name. In the latter case, juxtaposition of the names should be clearly specified.

Although the manufacturer cannot control the content of his customers' advertisements (even when part of a cooperative program), the arrangement should provide for appropriate use of the designer's name in any advertisement placed directly by the manufacturer or in promotional materials issued by the manufacturer. Often this is handled by making the form and content of advertisements, releases, and other materials subject to the designer's reasonable approval.

Other specifics that can and should be controlled by the arrangement are such matters as sales territory (perhaps the entire world or confined to the United States); price range (fabrics at no less than $4.50 and no more than $7.50 a yard, occasional tables at no less than $135 per unit); nature of market (only to department store and similar customers or only through decorative showrooms); and extent of sales term (two years plus a 90-day selloff period or indefinitely).

PROPRIETARY RIGHTS: LIABILITY

Proprietary rights to a specific design or group of designs can be either transferred to the manufacturer or retained by the designer. In the former instance, unless the arrangement carefully provides to the contrary, the manufacturer will be entitled to use the designs for any purpose and at any time. In the latter, subject to the manufacturer's right to use the designs for the specific purpose provided in the agreement, all other rights remain with the designer. For example, if a designer licensed a group of designs to a sheet mill for the production and sale of domestics, he or she could also license the same group of designs to a different manufacturer for the production and sale of upholstery fabrics or other noncompetitive products. A license confined to the United States would not prevent a separate arrangement with a foreign manufacturer for the production and sale of the identical merchandise in Europe or Japan.

Proprietary rights include the right to effect copyright or a design or mechanical patent, where applicable. Copyright or patent protection may not be obtainable in many instances (a reproduction desk, for example), but the agreement between the designer and the manufacturer should at least prevent that manufacturer from copying or imitating the designs either during or subsequent to the term of the arrangement.

With rights come responsibilities. The manufacturer is entitled to require the designer not only to confirm the originality of the designs but to stand behind them in the event of a claim that the designs infringe upon the proprietary rights of a third party. At the same time, the designer is entitled to require the manufacturer to stand behind the product and protect the designer from any third-party claim for personal injury or other damage arising out of a defective product. This is usually handled by the manufacturer adding the designer to its product liability insurance coverage.

EXCLUSIVITY

This can take any one of a number of forms depending upon the arrangement. It could be total, limiting the designer to a single manufacturer, even though the manufacturer's products are confined to a particular field, such as furniture. It could be by product, prohibiting the designer from creating fabric or like designs for a third party, but leaving the designer free in other fields such as furniture or table tops. It could be by category, prohibiting the designer to create domestics for any third party but without imposing any other restrictions.

It could be by design, prohibiting the particular design from being otherwise used for any purpose, while at the same time leaving the designer free to use other designs for any purpose including the same product category. It could be by sales market, prohibiting the designer from designing furniture for other manufacturers that intend to market it through retail outlets, while at the same time leaving the designer free to design identical types of furniture intended for the decorative market.

The important thing is that the agreement must clearly set forth the restrictions, if any, which the particular arrangement imposes on the designer.

COSTS

Preparation of design materials, particularly artwork, shop drawings, or models, is often a costly endeavor. Consequently where there is no commensurate fixed fee or minimum guarantee, the designer should try to have these costs paid by the manufacturer, even though the designer remains responsible for all aspects of design creativity and for the production of required materials. Other costs, whether for strikeoffs, samples, production, marketing, advertising, public relations, sales, and distribution, are normally the sole obligation of the manufacturer, and the arrangement should make that completely clear. Travel and maintenance costs incurred by the designer and his or her staff during the design and production process or for marketing and sales efforts should be reimbursed by the manufacturer.

MARKETING

The key to any successful program must be the marketing of the product line. Depending upon the nature of the market, the arrangement should provide for the manufacturer's commitment to specifically introduce products at a particular time or on an ongoing basis. This can involve presentations at wholesale markets, national or regional in scope, showroom presentation on a temporary or permanent basis, product brochures or catalogs, and other marketing materials. The manufacturer's obligations in these areas should be provided for in the arrangement, which should include as well the right of the designer to reasonably approve the method of presentation of the products at any show or showroom or in any brochure, catalog, or other material.

Equally important is for the arrangement to spell out the manufacturer's obligation to produce and distribute the product and regularly service customers purchasing it. Without such an obligation, a manufacturer could determine that initial orders were not sufficient to warrant any further effort. In such an event the designer's royalty compensation could prove to be virtually nonexistent.

TERMINATION

Particularly where the arrangement grants the manufacturer any form of exclusive rights, the terms of the arrangement should be limited either to a specific period of time or to an indefinite use of specific designs. In the former case, a time limit is essential where the designer intends to continue to design in a particular field even though his or her initial design arrangement is not renewed. Any manufacturer is loath to bring out a design collection in circumstances where a competitor can continue to market items created by the same designer.

Any term arrangement should contain a sell-off period, generally not longer than six months, during which the manufacturer is entitled to unload existing inventory including merchandise in the process of being produced at the date of termination. However, during such a selloff period the manufacturer is not to be entitled to undertake new production of that product. Termination can also apply to a particular design although the arrangement with the manufacturer continues in effect. For example, if the designer submits ten separate designs and after initial sampling the manufacturer decides to produce only six of them, all design rights to the unused four should immediately revert to the designer. Similarly, if an item is in fact produced and marketed for a period of time and is then withdrawn by the manufacturer from the market, the design rights to it should revert to the designer. If the manufacturer violates the contract in any material fashion, all proprietary rights should revert to the designer.

This overview of what is required in a product design arrangement does not deal with the many provisions common to any form of commercial agreement (such as arbitration, governing law, notice, or waiver), but it should expose the interior designer to all the elements that require consideration when entering the product design area. It should be evident that pro-fessional legal and accounting advice should be sought before the interior designer finalizes any arrangement in this field.

Relations with Trade Sources

In the past, the three parties involved in making an interior were the patron, the artisan, and the interior designer, who was called something else—perhaps artist-decorator like Louis Comfort Tiffany, architect like the Adams brothers, or cabinetmaker like Thomas Chippendale. The designer executed virtually everything he designed. What his own workroom couldn't produce—for instance, the rugs—he did not discuss with the patron.

Today the principals are the client, the trade sources, and the interior designer. The most striking change has been the development of what we call the *trade sources*—the multitude of manufacturers, wholesalers, dealers, service craftsmen, and contractors geared to work in tandem with interior designers primarily or exclusively (the ideal). They supply the manufactured or custom-made furniture, fabrics, floor coverings, accessories, lamps, lighting fixtures; they sew the draperies; they upholster; they apply fireproofing and other protective treatments to fabrics and dye them; they do the carpentry, the painting, the electrical wiring; they install the floor coverings—and so forth. They, in short, are the reason the design firm with extensive workshops of its own has become the exception rather than the rule. After he or she leaves the drawing board, the typical interior designer of today behaves more like a specifier and purchaser and less like a producer than in the past though he or she produces *custom* results—individualized interiors. The surprising speed with which he or she can do this depends on the flexibility and efficiency with which the designers and the trade sources have learned to work with each other.

Each design firm has to establish working relationships with trade sources on its own in accordance with the customs of the field, which have evolved for many good reasons. The nature and importance of that relationship are significantly affected by the geographic location of the designer's firm and the kinds of sources he or she uses.

Trade sources are not distributed evenly throughout the country; they are concentrated in major market centers. The acceleration in the growth of the older market centers, together with the opening of a great number of newer ones, are impressive indicators of the growth of what we might call the interiors industry. The most important of these centers are in New York, Chicago, Los Angeles, San Francisco, Dallas, Atlanta, and Miami, with newly developing and growing centers in a number of other cities throughout the United States and Canada. They consist of convenient clusters of showrooms displaying every conceivable type of furnishings for the interior design market. You may locate these centers through the various trade publications. Trade source information may also be obtained from local chapters or the national offices of ASID and IBD.

Designers based within a few hours of such centers enjoy tremendous advantages and conveniences:

1. Continual and effortless awareness of new trends and products.

2. Relative freedom from dependence upon their own stocks of samples and library of catalogs and manufacturers' literature.

3. Ease in comparative shopping for prices as well as product availability.

4. Freedom from costly, time-consuming travel with or without clients to research the market for specific jobs.

5. A wealth of custom manufacturers and services such as fabric workrooms and cabinetmakers to choose from close at hand.

6. Lower freight and delivery charges.

Designers far from major market centers must operate a little differently:

1. They must maintain and absorb the cost of more inclusive libraries of samples, catalogs, and manufacturers' reference material.

2. They are more apt to find it convenient to carry an inventory of floor samples and even

stock, which in turn can lead naturally into a retail business conducted with interior design service, rather than an interior design operation alone.

3. They should travel periodically to market centers to keep in touch with trends and new products.

4. Because of the additional expenses entailed by the first three points, they should be careful to choose fee bases and markups that cover the extras realistically.

In developing a working relationship with trade sources, the designer should be aware of the following factors: *credit, purchasing information,* and whether the trade source operates a *closed showroom.*

CREDIT
Without credit, the lifeblood of our economy would cease to flow, for credit is the network of vessels that enables the sustaining fluid of goods and services to circulate. The designer extends credit to his clients and in order to do so needs credit from his trade sources. Their willingness to extend it and under what terms is based upon his ability to establish a credit standing when starting a business and to maintain it throughout his career.
    Credit is established by:

A. Registering with the three credit agencies (listed below).

B. Establishing a good record in trade relations.

Let's discuss these two points in detail as follows.

A. REGISTERING WITH THE THREE CREDIT AGENCIES

1. Dun & Bradstreet. The best known and most universally used source of credit information, it maintains current credit information on all types of businesses.

2. Lyon Furniture Mercantile Agency. This credit agency is best known within the furniture world. It is used intensively and primarily for organizations that operate shops and maintain inventory. It also registers interior designers and is used as a source of financial information by the manufacturers and managers of wholesale showrooms.

3. Allied Board of Trade. This organization describes itself as "the official registration and credit bureau for the Decorative Furniture Manufacturers' Association and as a credit center for the Drapery, Upholstery, and Allied Decorative Trades." It is concerned only with the interior design field and to that purpose:

a. Publishes its *Credit Green Book,* which lists the names of approximately 12,000 active designers and summarizes each one's financial condition and suggested credit. The *Credit Green Book* is used by the sources as a handy credit guide and also to some extent to verify a prospective purchaser's claim that he is in fact a professional interior designer.

b. Issues to each listed designer an identification card that identifies the designer to trade sources.

c. Provides other pertinent information to the field in general and a direct-mail service for a fee.

The Allied Board of Trade, unlike the other two agencies, has restrictive provisions for registration to inform the trade that the designers listed have given proof of:

a. Meeting minimum professional standards for scholastic training.
b. Meeting minimum professional standards for practical training and experience.
c. Being in business with:
    (1) A record of past trade relations.
    (2) A sales tax number (if in a sales tax area).
    (3) Stationery, billheads, office forms.

Registration with any of the credit agencies gives the trade sources a quick reference on which to check a designer's request for credit. New design organizations, especially those in major market centers, may find it very helpful to register with the Allied Board of Trade; its identification cards are particularly useful in opening showroom doors, since they are accepted as definite proof that the designers holding them are producing members of the profession.

A designer's failure or inability to provide reassuring financial information to a trade source may force him or her to purchase goods on a COD basis, to order custom-made items pro forma, or to leave large deposits. Beginners may find they have to do any or all of these things to get themselves started, working at first with a limited number of sources until those sources begin to extend credit to them. The next step is to use those sources as credit references in applying for credit from new sources. This brings us to the second method for establishing credit.

B. ESTABLISHING A GOOD RECORD IN TRADE RELATIONS

The designer who pays trade source bills promptly will find that fact is readily given to new sources that inquire about him or her. A poor record leaps through the grapevine even faster; that is, the designer's record and his or her rating are identical. However, credit is not the only thing the designer can lose when his or her rating drops. He also falls to the bottom of the list for every kind of service and courtesy—the placing of orders, deliveries, adjustments. The designer who pays bills promptly is assured not only of credit but of the little extra attentions and considerations that oil the wheels of his or her operation. Maintaining a good credit rating pays dividends.

PURCHASING INFORMATION

One of the most crucial necessities for a happy relationship between designers and trade sources is clarity in purchase orders and specifi-
cations, so that such matters as dimensions, completion and delivery dates, and other facts needed for the satisfactory manufacture and delivery of the order are not subject to misinterpretation. Purchasing information can be relayed through

1. Purchase orders

2. Other specifications

3. Consultations with craftsmen

4. Changes in purchase specifications

5. Adjustments

6. Delivery dates

Each of these points will now be discussed.

1. PURCHASE ORDERS

The preparation and use of purchase orders were covered in Chapter 15. To restate the basic principle: it is essential to clearly identify the item to be bought and to clearly describe what is to happen to it. If this is done, the designer *should* expect the source to deliver properly or else be accountable for mistakes. Proper purchase orders eliminate one of the most annoying sources of irritation in the field.

2. OTHER SPECIFICATIONS (INCLUDING MEASUREMENTS, WORKING DRAWINGS, AND SO ON)

In major market centers it is unusual to find a designer operating even his or her own drapery workshop, and in more isolated locations, it is even rare to find a design organization completing all its work as a self-contained unit with its own craftsmen. Even where the designer controls the work in his or her own shop, a proper work program requires care in making and checking specifications. But it is much more essential when the orders go to many outside workshops. In such cases something else is needed beside clarity in the measurements and specifications: it is also essential that orders and items be clearly identified and keyed since each shop—that of the contractor, the carpenter, the painter, the electrician, the cabinetmaker, upholsterer, and so on—is always awash with orders from many different designers.

3. CONSULTATIONS WITH CRAFTSMEN

The designer should ask the craftsman to estimate the cost of special work so that it can be figured into the budget. This will eliminate any possibility of disagreements over unanticipated labor costs after jobs have been completed. Similarly, the designer should consult with the craftsman or technician in order to prepare specifications properly if he or she has any doubts about such things as construction details, drapery measurements, electrical work, or the like. Cooperating from the beginning prevents the discovery of problems after it is too late.

4. CHANGES IN PURCHASE SPECIFICATIONS

Changes in job site conditions that may develop as a project moves along occasionally necessitate changes in purchase orders and specifications already placed with a source. A designer cannot expect the source to bear the resulting financial burden (and if the designer took proper care with the letter of agreement or contract, as covered in Chapters 8, 12, and 22, he or she will also be protected). But the source can help the designer in expediting such changes. Where the source has not yet begun to process the order, there should be no penalty to any member of the eternal triangle—designer, client, source. If changes are called for as a result of measurements or specifications computed by the source, there should be no question that the liability lies with the source. If changes are required as a result of the source's incorrect interpretation of properly prepared specifications, there again should be no question of the source's liability. In the last two cases, it is up to the source to make good at its own expense.

5. ADJUSTMENTS

While in the preceding paragraph we discussed adjusting to changes in the premises, here it is financial adjustments called for by imperfections or inadequacies in the product supplied by the source. If such inadequacies become apparent, the designer has the right to expect the source to cooperate toward an equitable settlement, and the good, prompt-paying customer will find his or her source more responsive. The designer should also be aware that on occasion the source may properly give formal notification that it does not guarantee the performance of certain goods from the standpoint of durability or similar factors; for instance, such disclaimers frequently appear on the tags of luxurious but fragile fabrics.

6. DELIVERY DATES

The timing of delivery is one of the essential factors in a successful installation. The adherence to delivery dates by sources has long been a nettlesome problem. Generally the client specifies an installation date when client and designer agree to proceed with the job, and it is good business to meet this date or come reasonably close to it. As to the role of sources in making it possible for the designer to meet the installation date by delivering orders on time, there is no doubt that complications can and do arise which make it impossible for a source to meet a promised date; that is understandable. However, it also happens that certain sources glibly give assurances about dates when they know that their backlog or other conditions will prevent timely delivery. It is imperative that as the designer learns by experience, he or she avoids sources that have proven to be unreliable. It is better to work with a source that gives a realistic date and lives up to it than with a source that will promise anything to get the order and then leave the designer out on a limb, with a frustrated client threatening to saw it off.

THE CLOSED SHOWROOM

The growth of concentrated showroom centers where trade sources present a tremendous array of merchandise to the professional interior designer is a result of the tremendous social and economic role that the design professional has assumed. As a stimulus to sales and to the designer's imagination—and certainly as a convenience—the manufacturers' and representatives' showrooms in these concentrated centers are an enormous boon to all concerned.

Since the qualified designer must protect the professionalism of the field, he would do well to give careful consideration to the practices of the showrooms he intends to patronize. Because of the mutual interdependence of the profession and the trades, they both have everything to gain by mutual cooperation in sound business conduct.

Theory, Objectives, and Methods of Recording Time

Though the interior designer appears to be engaged in the sale of tangible merchandise—furnishings, accessories, and so on—this, of course, is not what he or she sells in actuality. Every sale or purchasing suggestion depends upon the professional competence and time needed to create an interior, so the commodities that the designer really sells are these intangibles—*talent* (with the other components of professional competence) and *time.* These commodities are extremely hard to measure in terms of dollar compensation. It is in fact impossible to suggest a perfect formula for arriving at a just price for professional proficiency. But it is not impossible to find ways of measuring time and of computing its value.

The attitudes about the usefulness of recording time that prevail today among interior designers seem to follow three distinct patterns:

1. Where designers are accustomed to billing clients for time, the need for a time-recording system is assumed as a matter of course.

2. Where designers are attuned to the idea of compiling statistical information about their own practice for future guidance, the need for a time-recording system is also assumed as a matter of course.

3. With no direct motivation, other designers see no need at all for maintaining time records. This group constitutes the vast majority of designers heading small or one-person organizations. Such firms as a rule give little or no consideration to time as a component of the costs that the firm invests in a job. Their typical procedure on a residential job is to work on a retail or markup basis without thinking about the relationship of the time spent on the job to the profit that results. They do not ask themselves what the earnings represent in terms of time expended. Did they work for $1 an hour, $5 an hour, or what? They do not relate the time eaten up by difficult or garrulous clients to their profit margins. This attitude is both unbusinesslike and unprofessional. It takes intel-

ligence to run a practice successfully, and this intelligence has to be applied to a shrewd study of all the big and little wheels that make an office run efficiently.

WHY RECORDING TIME IS IMPORTANT

Recording time is an important factor to consider because the information it yields enables a firm to:

1. RELATE TIME TO QUOTING A FEE BASIS FOR A NEW JOB

If time records of jobs have been kept, they will indicate the amount of time needed to complete a variety of jobs under a variety of conditions resulting in a variety of profit margins. Assume, for example, that a potential client appears with a modest budget to do three rooms. With the budget as a base, the designer can roughly determine the size of the possible gross profit. By checking previous jobs, the designer can estimate how many hours this kind of job has required in the past. Then, by dividing the average number of hours into the average gross profit, he can determine what approximate hourly return he can expect and whether to take the job or not. Similarly, if a potential client wishes to work on a flat-fee basis, the designer can refer to the results of previous jobs, find jobs with a reasonable degree of similarity, and quote a fee estimate that makes sense.

2. RELATE TIME TO THE PROGRESS OF EACH CURRENT JOB

A periodic review of the time being spent on current jobs can be a revealing eye-opener on profitable and unprofitable procedures. With an estimate of the predictable gross profit of any given job based upon an analysis of its scope that was made when he accepts the job, the designer is in a position to know how much time it pays him to give the client. If the time records indicate an abnormal amount of time spent dealing with a difficult personality, they cue the designer to inform the client that either

a. Time must no longer be wasted.

b. Or the designer will begin to charge for the extra time expended on the job. In fact some design firms routinely provide for the shilly-shally hazard when they quote a retail or markup basis for the fee on a residential job. They do this by adding a provision that the fee basis allows a specific number of shopping hours and that if additional hours are required, they will be charged to the client at an hourly rate. The system is an excellent deterrent to hemming and hawing clients wasting valuable time and illustrates the value of recording time even in residential work where fees are based on the cost of merchandise.

The principle of relating time to the progress of current jobs also applies to jobs undertaken on a flat-fee basis. It is essential that the designer keep a record of time expended as he or she progresses with the job. Should conditions arise that slow his work not only on the drawing board, but in discussions with the client or workers and in solving problems of installation or delivery, keeping tabs on the time used up will prevent him from losing track of the situation and alert him early enough that he must speed up some of the work if he is to avoid an inadequate hourly return on the job. Peculiarly enough, this kind of information is relatively more beneficial to the smaller design firm than the larger one. Unproductive or wasted time is more apt to occur during jobs done by designers whose staffs are small or who work alone—the designers who can least afford to waste their energy.

3. RELATE TIME TO THE COMPLETED JOB AND THE PROFIT EARNED FROM IT

It has been suggested in previous chapters that jobs can very easily be analyzed for costs, selling price, and gross profits through the maintenance of some form of inventory control sheet. If the designer also maintains a time record for each job, he or she will have an immediate picture showing the relationship of the profit to

the time expended. This information can then be related to:

a. The hourly return earned.

b. The design firm's ability to complete a job profitably.

c. The productivity of individual staff members.

d. A record of job costs and profits to be used for future guidance.

4. RELATE TIME TO BILLING IF THE LETTER OF AGREEMENT CALLS FOR SUCH CHARGES

If the working arrangements with a client call for any type of time-charge billing, it is imperative that time records be accurately maintained. This is necessary not only for the primary purpose of accumulating time for billing to the client, but for providing corroborative records in the event time charges are questioned. You can take it for granted that somewhere in the progress of a job in which time is a billing factor, the client will question the charges. The designer must be in a position to substantiate the time billing by referring to time records that indicate the date, the number of hours expended, and a description of the services performed.

5. RELATE TIME TO THE PRODUCTIVITY AND ACTIVITIES OF EMPLOYEES

By the very nature of his or her work, the typical interior designer must move about a great deal, visiting clients, job sites, the workshops where craftsmen must be supervised and, of course, shopping. Design firms that employ staff designers must maintain a reasonable degree of control over such employees' activities. A review of their activities will indicate the productivity of individual employees, as well as the relative profit of various activities. Since employee salaries are a major item in the overhead of a design office, it is essential to relate the cost of an employee to his or her productivity. Many firms observe employee activities with deep concern and maintain records of each employee's income productivity along with his or her time productivity, periodically reviewing them for profitability and efficiency.

VALUATION OF TIME

If time billing is to be a factor in an interior designer's fee basis and if time recording is to be a factor in maintaining statistical and historical records, then a dollar basis for charging time must be developed. The cost basis for time charges breaks down into two distinct categories:

1. The charge for the principal's time.

2. The charge for employees' time.

Each of these will be discussed as follows.

1. THE CHARGE FOR THE PRINCIPAL'S TIME

The time charge for the principal of a firm or for an individual interior designer practicing alone must be evaluated differently from the time charge for an employee. The following factors must be considered:

a. Geographic location. The geographic region where the designer's office is located has a bearing upon the attitude of clients toward time charges. In some parts of the country a charge of about $50 per hour is taken by clients in stride; in other areas clients look askance at such a rate and indeed at the very idea of time charges.

b. Economic status of clients. The economic habits, standard of living, and financial resources of the clients, their community, and their particular social circle have a decided bearing both on the size of time rates and on the use of time charges.

c. Availability. The availability of the designer to accept work has a tremendous bearing on

what he computes the value of his time to be. The designer who is in demand can certainly think in terms of a much higher hourly time rate than the designer who is hungry for work.

d. Competition. The time charges customarily set by competing designers in the same locale will affect the terms that any designer can safely demand without risking the loss of potential clients.

e. Anticipated earnings. Designers with little confidence in their potential earnings are happy to make anything in the way of income, while others will set their goals on what they consider a decent income to be and adjust their time charges accordingly. To do that, the designer must keep his overhead expenses in proportion to his anticipated earning capacity.

There is no arbitrary formula or rule of thumb that can be counted on to devise a chart of time charges for any given designer. However, finding the most advantageous, acceptable charge can be derived through:

a. An analysis of the conditions described above.

b. Maintenance of time records to cover all types of work performed by the designer and a comparison of the time expended for each job with the profit earned. From this, the value of time for different kinds of jobs can be computed.

c. A calculation of how much needs to be earned to cover overhead and the designer's income. For example, if, in a one-person firm, the annual overhead is $15,000 per year and the designer sets $25,000 as his or her annual income and if one assumes as is customary, that a principal has about 1,500 productive hours a year, a rate of between $25 and $30 per hour is arrived at (by dividing 1,500 hours into $40,000 or the total of overhead and income). This figure should be compared with the results of earlier jobs described in the previous paragraph.

All too often an hourly amount is commonly accepted as a base rate as a result of discussions among interior designers at professional conferences. Frequently its only basis is sheer repetition. This rate should not be used blindly. It is always essential to review the factors itemized above.

Principals in larger design organizations can set any hourly charges they feel are compatible with their reputation and availability and the type of client. Principals in the larger firms have many duties other than designing, and each person's time may be divided into many areas. Thus, there is no formula for determining all charges. Most nationally known designers work on a basis of between $50 and $100 an hour. It is not essential to attempt an accurate evaluation of a principal's time in larger organizations because measurable income is produced basically by the efforts of the staff, and the productive value of the principal's supervision is too nebulous to compute.

2. THE CHARGE FOR EMPLOYEES' TIME

Time charges for the productive hours of the staff—designers, draftsmen, shoppers, job captains, office managers, and so on—can be determined through specific computations.

There are approximately 235 productive days in a year, after Saturdays, Sundays, holidays, vacations, and average sick leave are eliminated. Translating productive days into hours, we find that at seven hours a day, we have 1,645 potentially productive hours per employee. This should be further reduced by deducting 5 percent of that time for coffee breaks, trips to the water cooler, and so on, leaving 1,563. If an employee earns a yearly salary of $15,000, the hourly cost is then $9.60. The markup basis of billing time can thus lead to definite and accurately calculated charges.

The markup rate that has been arrived at in general practice by a consensus of experienced firms is that hourly cost should be multiplied by 3. The selling price for the time of the $15,000-per-year employee is $28.80 (3 times $9.60). A chart should be prepared for each employee (or classification of employee) indicating the basic cost and billing price for each hour of each type of an employee's time. The importance of such a chart in the development of residential fees should be obvious and even more so in determining compensation in nonresidential work.

FORMS FOR RECORDING TIME

To record time for whatever reason—either for billing clients or for compiling statistical information—a system should be instituted and followed. The system and its results will be only as accurate as the people who have the responsibility of recording their time. If either the principals or staff members are careless about recording time, then the results are worthless. To enable a design firm to record and assemble time information smoothly, the following forms are suggested—to be used either as they are shown here or as a base from which to set up forms suitable to particular offices.

EXHIBIT A

Exhibit A is a weekly time sheet using a code to indicate the type of work the staff member performed. The staff member (or principal) records the name of the client or clients served, the time spent, and the areas of work on a daily basis. From such information the employee's overall productivity for the week can be determined.

EXHIBIT B

Exhibit B is a job-time accumulation form showing the time spent on each job. The entries are made from Exhibit A by posting the time to the division that coincides with the code used. As the job proceeds, the designer should maintain a running total of each column, giving him or her a complete and up-to-date picture of where the job is going in terms of time use. The designer should note at the top of the form any information that pertains to time billing or limitations in the time allowed or the time billable for that job. At the completion of each job, all columns should be totaled to determine the total number of hours worked. This information can then be tied in with other items of income and cost to determine the profitability of each job.

EXHIBIT C

Exhibit C is one type of daily time sheet; it is an excellent example of recording in detail what work has been done and whether the time is chargeable. In addition it records expenses incurred for the job that might or might not be chargeable to the client.

Columns 1–3	Identify the client.
Column 4	Indicates the phase of the job (if the job is broken down into phases).
Column 5	Describes the work done. This information is invaluable if there is time-charge billing.
Column 6	Records the number of hours spent from what hour to what hour (time should be recorded to the nearest quarter hour).
Column 7	Indicates whether the time is chargeable or not.
Column 8	Records expenses incurred by the designer.
Column 9	Indicates whether the expenses are chargeable to the client.

EXHIBIT D

Exhibit D is a job-time accumulation form used in conjunction with Exhibit C, the daily time sheet. Exhibit C describes time right down to recording whether it has been billed or not. If time is billable, it is entered under "Chge" as PR for principal or ST for staff. When the time is billed, the invoice number and date of such billing are entered in the last two columns, thus allowing complete control.

Each design firm should first analyze what in-

formation it wishes to accumulate and to what degree it wishes to control time before selecting a time-recording system. After a designer decides about its time requirements, it is a simple matter to devise a system based upon variations of the two sets of forms shown here.

A

Weekly Time Sheet

Employee _____   Week Ending _____

Key to be used: C   — Conference   Ex-O — Expediting & Ordering
                  D-R — Designing & Rendering   Es   — Estimating
                  Sh — Shopping   D   — Drafting
                  S   — Supervision

Job	Monday	Tuesday	Wednesday	Thursday	Friday	Saturday	Total
Other Time*							

* Other time is that time which cannot be charged directly to any definite job.

Form No. 14 (To obtain forms, see page 4.)

B

Job Time Accumulation

Job

Employee	Conference	Drafting	Designing and Rendering	Estimating	Shopping	Expediting and Ordering	Supervision	Other

Form No. 15 (To obtain forms, see page 4.)

C

Daily Time Sheet

Name: _____

Date: _____

Checked By: _____

Entered By: _____   Date: _____

Form # Job #	Client/Company	Project	Ph.	Assignment or Conference	Hours	Chg.	Expenses					Charge to
							Travel	Amt.	Sub.	Amt.	BP	
①	②	③	④	⑤	⑥	⑦	—		⑧		—	⑨

Form No. 16 (To obtain forms, see page 4.)

D

Client Time Record

Entered By

Job No. _____
Name: _____
Add: _____
Rate—Pr. _____ Staff _____

Date	Staff	Phase	Area	Code	Detailed Explanation	Hrs.	Charge Pr.	St.	Inv. No.	Date

Form No. 17 (To obtain forms, see page 4.)

Insurance

In the course of daily affairs, every businessperson is constantly exposed to potential liabilities and hazards, most of which never develop. But when the unexpected catastrophe—fire, injury, robbery, claims of negligence, or so on—strikes, the lack of protective insurance can be a disaster. It is virtually impossible for a small business or even a large one to carry enough insurance to protect it against every possible eventuality; the cost would be prohibitive. The average businessperson probably knows less about the intricacies of insurance than of any other single business element he or she has to contend with. It is therefore necessary to retain a reputable insurance counselor, preferably one familiar with the business problems specific to the interior design field.

The first step in the development of a sound insurance program for an interior design firm is a discussion among the insurance counselor, the accountant, and the principals of the firm who are most familiar with the present and future plans of the operation. The preliminary discussion should include what the insurance counselor sees as the potential hazards from a property insurance standpoint, as well as from a liability insurance standpoint, as they pertain to the designer's business. Obviously, the scope of the suggested program will vary with the size, complexity, and needs of each particular firm, in addition to its ability to pay for insurance.

The following description of insurance coverage has been developed to explain insurance needs and how they relate to the designer's activities.

A. REQUIRED INSURANCE
The insurance counselor should point out that the following kinds of insurance are a *must* for interior designers.

1. PROPERTY INSURANCE
This form of protection will protect your building (if you own it), the improvements and betterments you have made to a rented building,

your furniture, equipment, and machinery, as well as your stock. Also the policy may be extended to include those items that do not belong to you, but that are held in your possession, such as the property of clients or goods on consignment. It is important for the insurance counselor to guide the designer in the selection of coverage on either a "named peril" or an "all-risk" basis. The difference is that the former only provides coverage for those perils specifically stated, such as fire, lightning, or wind storm, whereas on the all-risk basis, protection is much broader and will be covered for "everything," except those items specifically excluded, such as wear and tear or war.

2. LIABILITY INSURANCE
Designers are not only liable for their own acts or claims of negligence, but they may also be liable for the work, products, and activities of their contractors and suppliers over whom they have no performance control. For these reasons it is imperative that the counselor point out the various forms of third-party coverage protection.

a. Liability insurance may include bodily injury and/or property damage said to have been done or caused by your negligence.

b. Product liability insurance will protect you in the event of bodily injury and/or property damage caused after you have relinquished possession of a product or a subcontractor has done so on your behalf. This is an extremely important coverage and could include such items as, for example, a claim where your carpenter has left the premises and a child of your client is severely cut by a medicine cabinet that falls out of the wall. Although your subcontractor is primarily liable, your products and completed operations insurance will provide excess protection.

c. Liability insurance also includes coverage in the event that an independent contractor does not have valid and collectible insurance after a claim and the claimant includes you along with the contractor. While the contractor has primary insurance and yours will be excess, if the contractor has no primary insurance, then yours takes over. At any rate, your defense will be paid by your insurance carrier.

3. PERSONAL INJURY PROTECTION
This is also a part of your liability policy and covers you in the event of an allegation of libel, slander, defamation of character, false arrest, invasion of privacy, wrongful eviction, and a few more torts.

4. PROFESSIONAL LIABILITY INSURANCE
This extremely important form of insurance is written specifically for the interior designer. No lawyer, doctor, or engineer would be in business without professional liability insurance, and neither should you be. This plan is sponsored by ASID, and we strongly suggest that you purchase an adequate amount of liability protection should you face an allegation of bodily injury and/or property damage alleged to have been caused by a professional misjudgment. The policy is extremely broad and would respond to such claims as failure to comply with regulation fire-retardant materials, errors or omissions in specification drawings, installation of erroneously ordered carpeting, and so on.

Your insurance counselor will point out, and the policy will state, that there is no coverage available if you overstep your bounds and delve into the domain of the architect and/or engineer.

5. AUTOMOBILE INSURANCE
Liability insurance, both bodily injury and property damage, as well as comprehensive and collision coverage, should be included in the prudent businessperson's portfolio. Nonowned automobile coverage—a very inexpensive form of protection—is extremely important and should be included. This provides protection to you in the event that an employee, while using his or her own car, has an accident while on or about your business. The claimant will undoubtedly include you in any action taken, and with this coverage, you will be protected.

6. UMBRELLA INSURANCE
This term identifies insurance that supplements the liability protection provided by automobile and general liability insurance contracts. It is extremely important protection, becoming more so each year, and should be part of the insurance counselor's analysis.

7. WORKMEN'S COMPENSATION INSURANCE
This is normally statutory in all states where a corporation has one or more employees, where a partnership has employees (other than the partners), or where a sole proprietor has employees (the sole proprietor is excluded).

B. OTHER AVAILABLE INSURANCE
The following coverages are *advisable* and should be thoroughly discussed with your insurance advisor.

1. PROCESSOR'S FLOATERS
Items that you take to subcontractors on behalf of your clients and that belong to your clients are your responsibility. These items may be properly protected on a broad basis by insuring the amount at risk at the various processors' or subcontractors' locations. It is usually a good idea to include flood insurance coverage at these locations.

2. VALUABLE PAPERS INSURANCE
This form of coverage protects you by paying for the time incurred to replace "valuable papers," that is, those drawings that have not yet been reproduced or are one of a kind. In the event of loss, funds are provided for duplication.

3. OPEN STOCK BURGLARY
If you purchase all-risk property insurance, then it is not necessary to buy open stock bur-

glary protection; this will already be included. However, if you do not have the all-risk protection, then you should have the burglary (of merchandise) protection.

4. ACCOUNTS RECEIVABLE INSURANCE
In the event of loss of accounts receivable records by fire or other insured perils, the insuror will pay for replacement of the records, as well as the difference between the amount of receivables you actually collect and the amount you should have collected in accordance with last year's figures for the same month, adjusted by the trend of business during the year.

5. CARGO INSURANCE
It is important to insure items that are being delivered to clients on vehicles which you either own or are being rented or leased to you. This form of protection will cover you if an insured peril happens to the items while they are being transported.

6. OCEAN MARINE INSURANCE
Many designers import items from Europe, Asia, Africa, or another far corner of the world. We strongly urge you to purchase adequate amounts of ocean marine insurance to properly protect your interest while the goods are in transit—sufficient to cover the imported item, plus freight, plus profit.

7. FLOOD INSURANCE
If you are in any way vulnerable to a potential flood, we strongly urge you to purchase this very inexpensive insurance from the federal government. Your insurance counselor will advise you on how to do it. If the amount of your exposure exceeds the amount available under the federal plan, your insurance counselor can help you protect the excess as well.

8. CRIME COVERAGES
Crime coverage comes in two categories: dishonesty and broad form money coverage. Dishonesty coverages are intended to protect you, the employer, from the dishonesty of employees. Broad form money coverage will protect you in the event of theft or disappearance of money other than because of the dishonesty of employees.

9. BONDS
Sometimes bid or contract bonds are required. The insurance company will guarantee the performance of the contract. It is, therefore, the underwriter's function to establish the firm's financial stability and credibility in order to issue the necessary bonds.

10. GROUP INSURANCE
Your insurance advisor should tell you about the types of group coverage available to you. They normally include life insurance, disability income, hospitalization insurance, and major medical coverage.

11. BUSINESS INTERRUPTION INSURANCE
In the event of a fire or other insured loss on your premises, this form of protection will replace the profit that you will lose as a result, as well as pay for continuing business and payroll expenses.

12. BUSINESS LIFE INSURANCE

a. A detailed study should be made of human risk factors, depending on whether your operation is conducted as a sole proprietorship, a partnership, or a corporation. You should find a way to provide continuity in the event of the death or disability of a principal or key person. Agreements, funded by insurance, should be drawn by your attorney to make these solutions work.

b. Profitable corporations should anticipate the retirement needs of both principals and employees and at the same time avail themselves of the tax breaks allowed through the installation of qualified pension and/or profit-sharing plans. Partnerships and sole proprietors should explore the liberalized advantages of HR-10 or Keogh plans.

The interior designer must recognize the hazards that his *own* business may create and select from this outline the types of insurance he most needs and can afford. It is essential that a firm's insurance program be reviewed periodically in the light of changes that may develop with the growth of the business. This can only be done by consulting the insurance counselor and making him or her aware of changes in the firm and its way of conducting business. Improper insurance coverage can be expensive when you consider the cost of unnecessary coverage and the damages a firm may suffer if insurance is lacking. That is why the selection of a competent and reliable insurance counselor is a serious responsibility.

The Client's Job Book

Every practicing designer knows and every designer-to-be learns that interior design is a vocation in which attention to detail is constant and the recording of details can become a monumental task. At worst it can become an all-enveloping obsession and a nightmare of gibberish, but at best it can be routinized into a smooth series of procedures that entail little worry and provide an immense amount of useful data, including statistical information for historical and financial analysis of the business.

Previous chapters have explained the need for routinized sequences in the planning of a job and the estimation of a client's budget. We have illustrated such procedures for ordering goods and services and controlling inventory, delivery, and billing. Since even a modest-sized job can easily entail the planning, purchasing, expediting, and installing of more than 100 different items of furnishing and service, it is essential to establish a cohesive record of the necessary information used during the job and for future reference. This record of information is the client's job book, maintained and continuously added to from the beginning to the end of the job.

SAMPLE JOB BOOK

On the following pages is a sample of a complete client's job book. At this point there is no need to review the forms, how they are prepared, or how they are used since all this has been fully covered in previous chapters. You can easily find your way from the floor plans and its code numbers identifying specific furnishings to the control sheets where the ordering of these items is recorded. On these sheets each item is fully described and illustrated by samples and pictures coded to the identifying number.

For example, on control sheet page 1, Drawing room page 1, item #4 shown in position on the room plan of Living room #2 is described as a Louis XV arm chair from JSC Furniture Co., using 2 yards of cord from JBS Trimming Co. and 1 yard of fabric from SMS Fabrics, with the purchase order numbers and the identifying code number keyed to the plan.

If you will turn to the section of the job book containing samples and pictures, you will find, under the heading of Drawing room, a picture identifying the Louis XV arm chair. You can then check the actual sample of the fabric to be used for this chair by referring to the page on Fabrics—Drawing room; in the lower left-hand corner of this page is the sample of the trimming for the same chair.

In essence, the client's job book is a complete record of all the designer's work in organizing an installation. Every interior designer must proceed in some fashion, through the processes of planning, scheduling purchases, and gathering samples. The key to functional smoothness in this sequence of tasks is not a folder or envelope bulging with loose scribbled notes, fabric samples, wallpaper, or carpeting, but a compact, neat, cross-referenced work book.

OTHER ADVANTAGES OF THE CLIENT'S JOB BOOK

A. It is immensely helpful in working with clients.
   1. Conferences with clients at any stage of the job go much more smoothly and require less of the designer's time if information is readily accessible and visually presented.
   2. The presentation of well-organized data can do much to enhance the designer's reputation for responsibility, stability, and reliability.
B. It ensures that information is available to the designer and the staff.
   1. Maintaining a client's job book can only result in smooth follow-through by assistants and other members of the staff.
   2. Instructions to assistants can be readily recorded and checked.
   3. In the event of the principal's absence, the work can be carried on without interruption.
   4. There is no great crisis if an employee

leaves the firm. Almost anyone else can pick up where he or she left off without too much trouble.

C. It is an almost infallible record for future reference.

1. If at any time in the future the client requests changes, additions, repairs, replacements, or perhaps repainting with a new color scheme, the designer has at his or her fingertips a complete, easily interpreted picture of the installation.

2. In undertaking new jobs for new or old clients, the designer will find that job books on completed jobs serve as handy resources to solve whatever problems come up as he or she struggles with new jobs. Reviewing old job books may remind him of points he might otherwise forget.

3. The job book, coupled with time records, cost records, and profit records, can be of invaluable assistance:

    a. In determining a fee or compensation base for a new job.

    b. In evaluating whether or not to continue to work with a client or take on new or additional jobs for the client. If the job book indicates that the client habitually makes many changes after accepting an original concept and if the time records indicate that an excessive number of hours were spent on the job, the designer has a real picture of the value of that client's business.

NOTES ON THE CLIENT'S JOB BOOK ILLUSTRATED HERE

This job book is a fair representation of what a completed book should look like. It is a complete working record of an actual job. However, the book from which these pages were taken is not as complete as many because it doesn't include a paint schedule or cost information. That is because the client's home had been painted shortly before the designer was hired, and the paint scheme was left alone. However, the preparation and use of a paint schedule are illustrated and described in Chapter 30, Other Working Forms.

Cost information was not recorded because the system used at the design office calls for all cost and income information to be kept in the bookkeeping and not in the design department. All that is required to complete the record is a summary of the following:

Total gross billing

Less: Total price costs

Gross profit

Total number of hours

Hourly return

Many design organizations use a more elaborate ordering control sheet, including three additional columns, as follows:

Cost of item

Retail price to client

Invoice number and date

This gives the firm a complete financial picture, in addition to providing control of the ordering process. The system was described in Chapter 14 with illustrated forms.

The job book illustrated here can be used as a guide by any design organization, large or small, simply by making additions or deletions to suit the circumstances of each particular firm.

Page 1. Control Sheet

Residence of
Room

Plan No.	Quantity	Item and No.	Firm	Ydge.	Fabric No.	Color	Firm	Finish	P.O. No.
1									
2									
3									
4	1	Louis XV arm chair 501/54	JSC	Cord 2 yds	# 09713	Yell & bl.	JBS		YB#8801
				Fabric 1 yd	#137195	yellow	SMS	Blue/str.yell	CH#8812

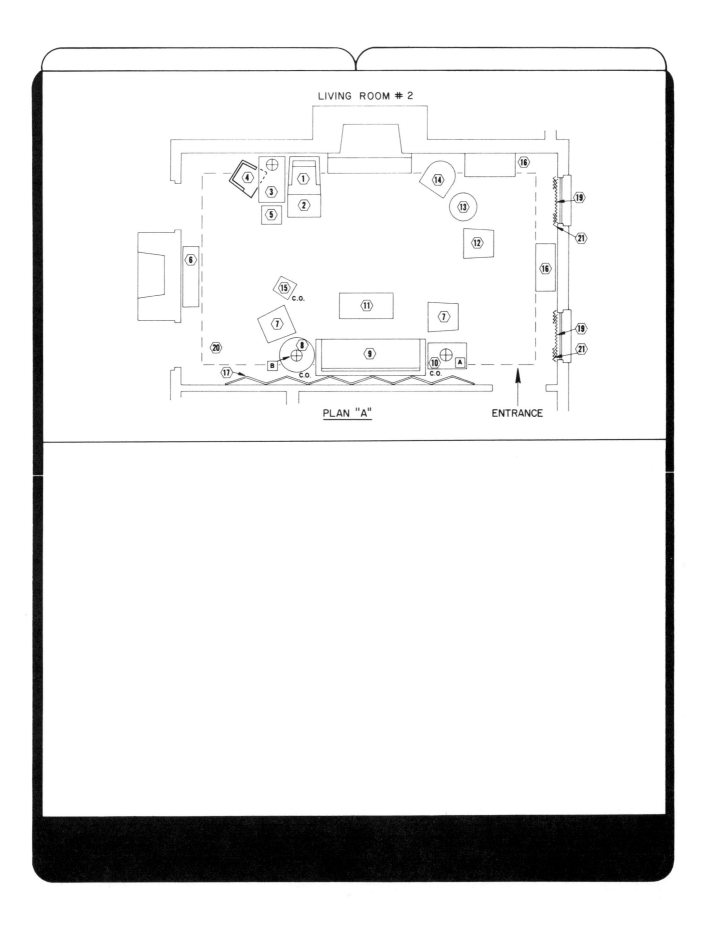

LIVING ROOM # 2

PLAN "A"

ENTRANCE

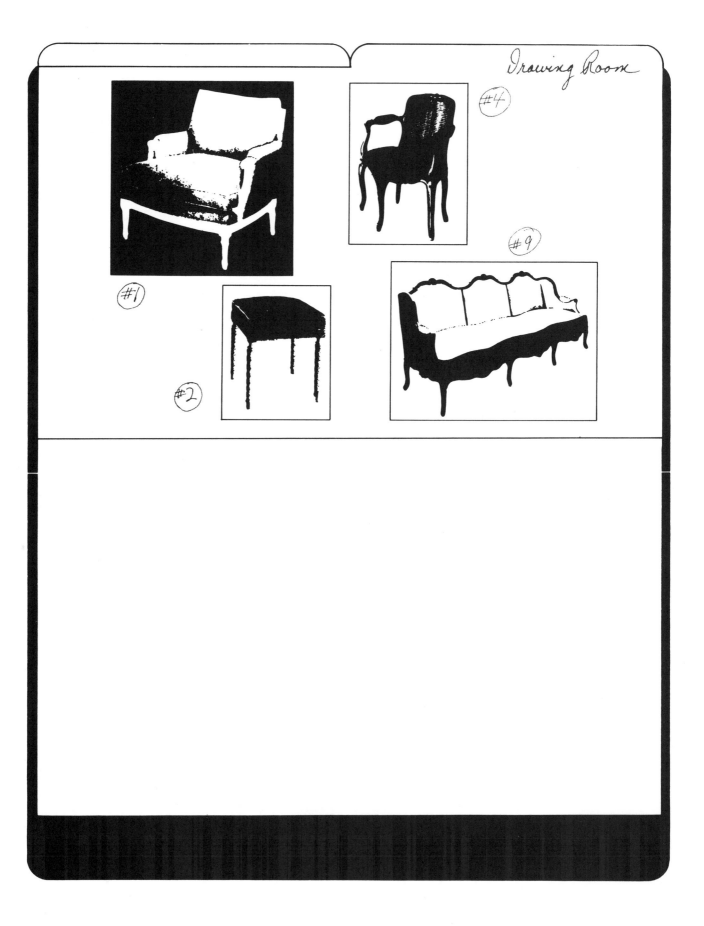

Drawing Room

#4

#9

#1

#2

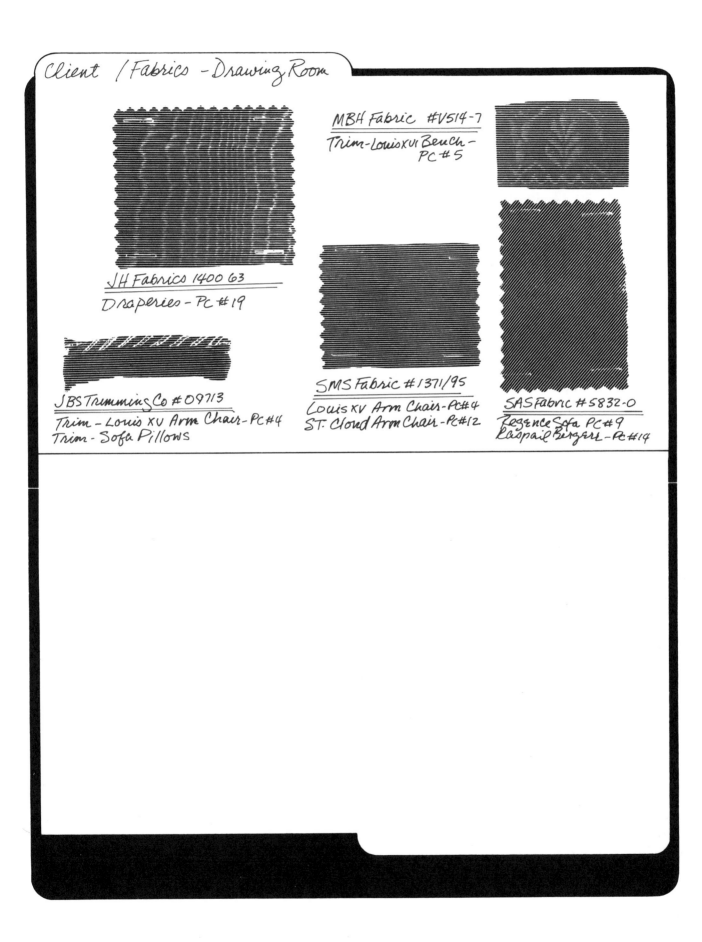

Client / Fabrics - Drawing Room

JH Fabrics 1400 63
Draperies - PC #19

MBH Fabric #V514-7
Trim - Louis XVI Bench -
PC #5

JBS Trimming Co # 09713
Trim - Louis XV Arm Chair - PC #4
Trim - Sofa Pillows

SMS Fabric #1371/95
Louis XV Arm Chair - PC #4
St. Cloud Arm Chair - PC #12

SAS Fabric #5832-0
Regence Sofa PC #9
Raspail Bergere - PC #14

CHAPTER 29

Contract Breakdown

The formal written instrument that defines and records the scope of the job, the precise responsibilities of designer and client, and the financial arrangements is the letter of agreement or professionally prepared contract described in Chapters 8 and 22. To abide by its numerous provisions requires constant rereading—a job that is not only time consuming but also unsatisfactory, since even the greatest alertness cannot prevent some costly lapse, a nerve-racking possibility. To avoid such uncertainties and time-consuming effort, a form called a *contract breakdown* should be used. It enables the firm to keep all pertinent details of the letter of agreement readily accessible and clearly defined and also makes it possible to keep track of progress as each phase of the job is carried out, so that nothing is forgotten or overlooked.

The contract breakdown form reproduced here is one that is in actual use in an interior design office and has stood the test of many years' application to a broad variety of jobs. A study of its provisions and of the completed form will indicate why it is worth the time to prepare it.

Before analyzing the information to be entered in the contract breakdown, let us note who performs the task, how many copies are made, and who receives the copies. It is either the principal of the firm or the individual responsible for negotiating the arrangements with the client who analyzes and breaks down the provisions of the letter of agreement in the contract breakdown form. The typed copies are duplicated for distribution to:

1. The principal: for observation and handy referral.

2. The job captain supervising the job and/or the job designer: to inform them of all pertinent facts about the agreement with the client. This alerts them of the need to promptly record the time and expenses put into the job and enables them to phase out the tasks and areas as each is completed. This breakdown of the component parts of the job is particularly invaluable if the job designer is responsible for controlling the cost of the job.

3. The bookkeeping department: for the control of billing and pricing. In some organizations the designer may do the pricing and the bookkeeping department the checking. But more often the bookkeeping department will do the pricing; a contract breakdown will give them all the information necessary to perform this task efficiently.

4. The secretary of the firm or similar executive-level employee(s) (depending upon the size and administrative organization of the firm).

The one- or two-person firm will find the contract breakdown form invaluable as a basic working tool to control the flow of information needed for the routine execution of all phases of each particular job. Keeping either a ready reference file of contract breakdowns of jobs in process or a contract breakdown form in each client's job folder takes the guesswork out of the working arrangements.

INFORMATION TO BE RECORDED

1. Job number (if the firm uses them).
2. Client's name and current address.
3. New address. The premises where the work is being done if the client is to move there at the completion of the job.
4. Name and address of client for billing purposes, with a notation of who is to receive the invoices and where they are to be forwarded.
5. Duplicate purchase orders. Does the client or another designated individual require duplicate purchase orders?
6. Special notes or requirements:
   a. Deposit information pertaining to confirmations.
   b. Contract minimum or information on the budget.
   c. Disposition of original deposit: whether refundable, applicable to purchases or to a fee, and so on.

A

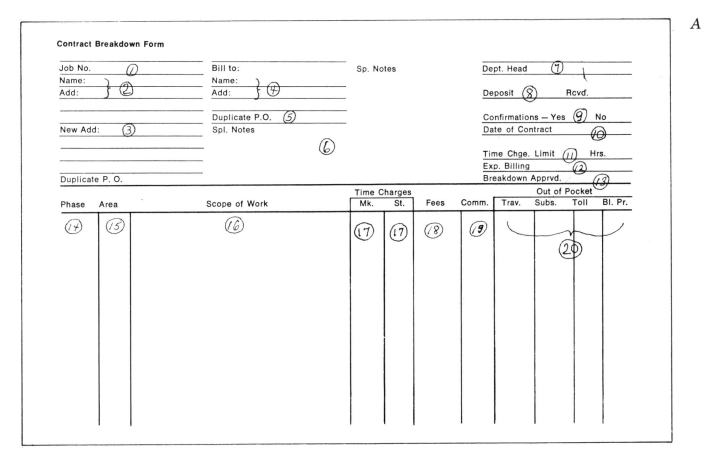

Form No. 13 (To obtain forms, see page 4.)

B

Contract Breakdown Form

Job No.	Bill to:
Name:	Name:
Add:	Add:
	Duplicate P.O.
New Add:	Spl. Notes
Duplicate P. O.	

Sp. Notes

1—Confirmations requesting deposits required on all purchases (other than fabrics, accessories, etc).
2—$5,000.00 minimum expenditure on contract.
3—Deposit of $1,000.00 is applicable to final bill if purchases exceed $5000.

Dept. Head

Deposit _____ Rcvd. _____

Confirmations — Yes X No

Date of Contract

Time Chge. Limit *None* Hrs.

Exp. Billing *Yes / Monthly*

Breakdown Apprvd.

Phase	Area	Scope of Work	Time Charges		Fees	Comm.	Out of Pocket			
			Mk.	St.			Trav.	Subs.	Toll	Bl. Pr.
I	ALL	Complete scaled layouts of furniture — to be approved by client. (NOTE: furniture layouts only)	NO	NO			Yes		Yes	.50¢ ea.
II	ALL	Purchases (other than floor coverings)	NO	NO	Retail					
III	ALL	Carpets & other floor coverings	NO	NO		25%				
IV	ALL	Interior painting (including schedules & supervision of all final coats)	NO	NO		15%				
V	ALL	Selection or specification of materials, equipment, hardware etc. as required for kitchens, pantries & bath.	NO	NO		15%				
VI	ALL	1 – Work executed by others but designed, detailed, selected or approved by_____ a—construction b—architectural alterations c—cabinet work	35.00	18.50						
		2 – Consultation with contractors or sub-contractors	35.00	18.50						
		3 – Designing specifications re: all construction or architectural work and alterations.								

Form No. 13

d. Any other information needed to guide the principal, the staff, or the book-keeping department not indicated elsewhere on the form.

7. Name of department head, job captain, or other individual in charge of the job.

8. Deposit. The amount of the required initial deposit and whether it has been received.

9. Confirmations. Are they to be sent to clients before ordering merchandise and services?

10. Date of contract or letter of agreement.

11. Time-charge limit. If the contract has a time-charge stipulation, this notation indicates whether there is a limit to the number of hours that will be paid for and, if so, what it is or whether all chargeable time expended will be charged.

12. Expense billing. This indicates whether the client is to be billed for expenses and the billing frequency.

13. Breakdown approval. After the contract breakdown is analyzed and prepared, it should be checked for correctness by the principal or other authorized individual.

14. Phase number. This is used to identify each separate phase of the job. Often the letter of agreement establishes the phase breakdown, and this column is for that information.

15. Area. For further control of the charges, the specific area of the job to which each item pertains is identified here.

16. Scope of work. Description of details to which various charges pertain.

17. Time charges made for
    PR (principal)
    ST (member of staff)
    These two columns indicate which phases of the work will be charged on a time basis and show the hourly rates for the principal and the staff.

18. Fees. This column indicates the fee basis for each particular type of work.

19. Comm. This column notes the phases of work that are subject to either commis-sions or markups and the rates to be charged.

20. Out of pocket. This is for recording job expenses such as for travel, subsistence, tolls, and blueprints and whether the client will or will not be charged for them.

A study of Exhibit B, a completed contract breakdown, illustrates the simplicity of its format, combined with its clarity as a concise checklist, enabling a busy office to control a job program through the routinized flow of information to all members of the responsible staff.

CHAPTER 30

Other Working Forms

Throughout this guide to business practices we have discussed the need for working forms and have shown examples indicating the procedures for a successful control of the flow of paperwork. In addition to those presented in other sections of this book, there are forms designed for various specific purposes, which can be adapted to the requirements of any office and can be very helpful in controlling operations, instructions, and records. Among them are

A. Transmittal letters
B. Purchase requisitions
C. Paint schedules
D. Change work orders
E. Drapery workroom checklists
F. Upholstery or reupholstery checklists
G. Sales invoices
H. Customer credit forms
I. Statements

Each of these nine points will be discussed below.

A. TRANSMITTAL LETTERS
During a job much information is shuttled between the designer's office, the client's office, and the offices of the various sources involved in the work. It is most important that some record be kept indicating that sketches, specifications, and other documents and instructions have been passed along. The letters of transmittal on pages 163 and 164 were designed to perform this function. Either can be made out by the designer in duplicate—one copy for his or her file and one copy to accompany the material. The use of such forms obviates the expensive and time-consuming necessity for dictating and typing repetitive letters. Examination and study of either form indicate its simplicity and the tremendous amount of information and control it provides with nothing more than a check mark.

It serves the additional purpose of keeping the designer alert to whatever information about the job needs to be passed along. Just looking at the form will bring key phrases and

conditions to his or her attention.

Essentially it is a time-saver, cutting the cost of communication and simplifying the maintenance of duplicate records for control purposes. The copy of the transmittal letter can be reviewed with a glance rather than by having to read and reread voluminous correspondence, and it protects the designer from the uncertainties of relying on the accuracy of the spoken word.

B. PURCHASE REQUISITIONS
The purchase order discussed in Chapter 15 represents an order placed by the designer directly with the manufacturer, supplier, or other trade source, in which case the designer assumes all liabilities attached to the placement of the order.

The purchase order requisition form may be substituted for the purchase order form under two conditions:

1. When it is necessary to establish that the requirements and liabilities of the order are being assumed by someone other than the designer. The need for such clarification occurs in nonresidential work when two distinct situations arise in jobs for big corporations and installations with very heavy purchasing requirements:
   a. Many large organizations have purchasing departments of their own and wish to do their own ordering and purchasing and to maintain their own control over these functions.
   b. The dollar amount of purchasing required may be so great as to (1) strain the designer's credit or (2) endanger the designer with tremendous liabilities. Such potential liabilities are very dangerous for small design firms. Should a problem arise in the relations of that eternal triangle of designer-client-source, the trade source will demand payment from whomever signed the purchase order. If the design firm issued its

Transmittal Letter

Company Name
Address

A

To: _____   Date: _____

_____

_____   Job: _____

Att: _____   Area: _____

We are sending you $\frac{\text{herewith}}{\text{under separate cover}}$ the following:

☐ Originals   ☐ Blue Prints   ☐ Photostats
☐ Samples   ☐ B & W Prints   ☐ Color Specifications
☐ Specifications   ☐ Shop Drawings

For:

☐ Estimate Only   ☐ Your Approval   ☐ Purchase Order #
☐ Your Information   ☐ Revisions   ☐ Approved as Shown

No. Copies	Dwg. #	Revised Date	Item

Copies To: _____   **Company Name**

By: _____

Form No. 18 (To obtain forms, see page 4.)

A

Transmittal Letter

Company Name
Address

To _____   Date _____

Address _____   Re: _____

_____   _____

_____   _____

Gentlemen:
We are sending you the following:

☐ Prints   ☐ Shop Drawings   ☐ Herewith   ☐ By Mail
☐ Specifications   ☐ Samples   ☐ Under Separate Cover   ☐ By Messenger

Drwg. No.	Latest Date	Copies Each	Description

These are sent   ☐ for approval/comments   ☐ per your request   ☐ for file
                        ☐ for correction   ☐ for coordination   ☐ for information
                        ☐ for estimating   ☐ for fabrication   ☐ _____

Remarks:
_____

_____

_____

_____

If this material is not received as listed above please notify us at once

Copies to: Yours very truly,
                                                  Company Name

_____

_____   by _____

Form No. 19 (To obtain forms, see page 4.)

Purchase Requisition No.

Company Name
Address _____

B-1

Source _____ Date

Address _____ Job No.

_____

Ship To _____

Address _____

_____

Client _____

_____ Area:

Mark For _____ Item No.:

Ship Via _____ When _____

Quantity	Number	Item	Color or Finish	Wood	Wholesale Per Unit	Wholesale Extended	Retail Per Unit	Retail Extended

Special instructions to be included on purchase order:

☐ For Resale
☐ Not For Resale

Company Name

Authorized By: _____

Form No. 20 (To obtain forms, see page 4.)

B-2

	Requisition for Purchase Order
Client	Date
Room	Due
Used For	

Company Name
Address

Ship to

To

Bill to

Attn: Tel.

Quant.	Details	Unit Price	Price	Unit	Charge

Purchase Order No.

Confirmation   By:

Form No. 21 (To obtain forms, see page 4.)

own purchase order, the designer would bear the liability; if the client issued the purchase order, the liability would be the client's.

Therefore, to allow the big corporate client the freedom of purchasing through its own organizations—and to pass the liability for purchasing to such a client—the designer should substitute a purchasing requisition (Form B-1) in place of a purchase order. The requisition spells out all the necessary details and instructions and is *sent to the client* to be transcribed onto the client's own purchase order form, signed by the client's purchasing agent, and forwarded directly by him or her to the trade source.

Ideally, this purchase requisition should be prepared in quadruplicate:

a. *White copy*. To the client or to whomever is doing the buying for the client.

b. *Pink copy*. To the client as a memo if the client has designated an independent buying agent.

c. *Yellow copy*. Retained by the designer or job captain.

d. *Blue copy*. For the client's folder.

2. When it is necessary to establish a flow of information between design staff and secretarial staff. In the larger organizations, designers must prepare purchase instructions. To expect them to sit down at the typewriter, carefully type out all the information, and then distribute the copies to the various departments for record control and mailing is a ridiculous waste of time and talent. All that should be required is for the designer to write out on duplicate carbon forms all the necessary purchasing specifications and information on a requisition for purchase order (form B-2). One copy is sent to the typist, who then prepares the complete purchase order and distributes copies according to set office routine, while the designer retains one copy for his or her own files.

The use of a formalized method of passing technical information to typists can be extremely helpful, not only in saving time, but in placing the responsibility for errors on the proper shoulders. This form takes the place of oral instructions and miscellaneous scraps of paper.

C. PAINT SCHEDULES

The proper application of paint colors to interior surfaces is one of the most integral phases in achieving the pleasant effects planned by the designer. However, since the designer cannot spend much of his or her time with painters and paper hangers (except perhaps to look over the painter's shoulder when the paint is first mixed), the instructions to the tradesmen must give concise information with minimal room for error.

The illustrated form sets specific instructions and treatments for each room and for the various parts of each room. Samples of colors are attached. Wallpaper samples may be similarly attached, though the fact that wallpaper is usually delivered to the job marked for a particular client and area makes this less necessary. (This wallpaper routine should be a normal procedure, as outlined in Chapter 15, Purchase Orders.) These forms should be prepared in duplicate with:

1. One copy for the craftsman.

2. One copy retained by the designer.

D. CHANGE WORK ORDERS

During a job that involves alterations, construction, electrical work, air-conditioning, and so on, changes may arise as a result either of existing conditions that were not discovered until work was begun or of requests by the client that necessitate changes in the original cost estimates and plans. The designer *should not* proceed with such changes unless he or she is specifically authorized to do so. The responsibility for incurring additional costs must be accepted by the client, otherwise the designer may be left

C

Company Name
Address

Paint Schedule

Residence of

_____

_____

_____

Room	Walls		Ceiling	Wood Work			
	Walls	Paper No.		Door Trim	Windows	Ceiling Mldg.	Base Board
UPSTAIRS SITTING ROOM	Paper	*Co. Name* Paisley wht/blk/ red	Paint Pale ice blue as existing ceiling	Paint door casings old red as paper	Paint white as ground of paper	Paint old red as paper	Paint old red as paper
	NOTE:	(1)	Paneling around fireplace breast, returns and mantel paint white as ground of paper. Cornice and base paint old red				
	NOTE:	(2)	Book cabinet and new doors of book cabinet paint white as paper				
BATH adjoining New sitting Room	Paper	*Co. Name* "New Paisley Blk/wht/ red	Paper	white as paper	white as paper	None	Tile
GUEST ROOM	Paint Putty	None	off white	off wht stripe putty	off wht	Putty	Putty
	NOTE:	Board and Batten paneling alcove paint off white Base and cornice in alcove paint Putty					

SAMPLES AND PAINT DESCRIPTIONS

Off White

Putty

Old Red

Form No. 22 (To obtain forms, see page 4.)

Change Work Order

Company Name
Address

D

Date _____

Client _____

Job _____

Location _____

Description of Change or Addition _____

_____

_____

_____

_____

_____

_____

_____

_____

_____

_____

_____

_____

_____

_____

_____

_____

_____

_____

_____

_____

_____

_____

Contractor's Cost _____

Signature of Contractor _____

Signature of Client's Representative _____

Signature of Job Captain _____

Form No. 23 (To obtain forms, see page 4.)

open to assuming the financial responsibility. In addition, the designer must pin down the source of additional changes made by the contractor.

When properly executed, the change work order will identify the changes and establish that the client and contractor have accepted such changes and the responsiblity for any resulting expense. This form should be prepared in quadruplicate:

1. One copy to the client.

2. One copy to the contractor.

3. One copy to the designer.

4. One copy to the bookkeeping department.

E. DRAPERY WORKROOM CHECKLISTS

In almost every interior design installation, the production of custom-made draperies, bedspreads, and other items will require that fabrics be purchased and sewn. The vast majority of interior designers do not have their own workrooms but rely on workshops that cater to the trade. Since draperies and curtains are almost invariably custom made for each specific installation (unlike furniture and many other items that are often purchased from standard stock), the designer must establish a good working system to eliminate errors and expedite the work.

We quote the presidents of two large drapery workrooms in New York:

1. The lack of cohesive information results in a tremendous waste of the designer's time in unnecessary telephone calls and trips to the workroom. If the designer prepares his basic instructions clearly, then the workshop is in a position to assist him in setting up efficient guides to the result he has in mind.

2. The modern drapery workroom is not only equipped to handle the fabrication of draperies and curtains but to assist the designer in arriving at the technical solutions that will ensure a better-than-good drapery installation and avoid costly errors and adjust-

ments—provided that the designer properly prepared basic information about his design intentions.

The drapery checklist is a basic outline of the information a workroom needs. The logical sequence of procedures is as follows: The information is brought to the workroom, then reviewed and interpreted, and the required services of the workroom are specified (that is, to take measurements, make estimates, and so on). The workroom should provide the designer with:

1. A written estimate for yardage required.

2. A written estimate for labor costs.

3. A written estimate for hardware and other costs.

4. Specification of the number of widths to be used in each pair of draperies.

F. UPHOLSTERY OR REUPHOLSTERY CHECKLISTS

Upholstery or reupholstery of furniture on a custom basis, when the designer is using a selected fabric and a selected trade workroom, raises almost the same questions and situations as exist with custom draperies. The designer should know what he or she wants to do with the furniture, how it is to be upholstered or changed, rebuilt, covered or recovered. Workrooms suggest that preparing information as outlined in the illustrated checklist, plus a conference with the workroom manager, will save the designer time and lessen the chance of errors. It is of interest to note that both drapery company presidents quoted above, who also operate as manufacturers of custom-upholstered furniture for the trade, indicate that checklists are inappropriate for upholstered furniture. Upholstered furniture is selected from stock models, and even in the interior design field there are manufacturers who will make no changes. In the case of custom upholsterers who do make changes, their procedure is to discuss such changes in detail, designating what proposals are workable and which are not. Based

Drapery Checklist

Company Name

E

Client _____   Date _____

Address _____

Installation Date _____

Room or Area _____

Type of Treatment: _____

_____

_____

_____

Repeat of Fabric _____

Width of Fabric _____

Extension of Draperies _____

	Yes	No
Measure To Be Supplied by Designer		
Measure To Be Supplied by Workshop		
Wall to Wall Carpeting		
Valance Type of Valance		
Ceiling to Floor		
Ceiling to Sill		
Ceiling to Apron		
Top of Trim to Sill		
Apron		
Floor		
Unlined		
Lined		
Lined & Interlined		
Trimmed		
Stationary		
To Draw		
Tie Back		

Hardware

Type _____

_____

_____

_____

_____

_____

Work Shop Estimate $ _____

Form No. 24 (To obtain forms, see page 4.)

F

Reupholstery Checklist

Company Name

Client _____   Date _____

Address _____

_____

Description of Furniture _____

_____

Style and Approximate Size _____

Repeat of Fabric _____

Width of Fabric _____

Type of Skirt _____

Type of Trim _____

Double Self Welt _____

Single Self Welt _____

Nail _____

Frame to be Tightened _____

Frame to be Touched Up _____

Change Seat Cushion   Yes ☐   No ☐

Description of Charge _____

_____

_____

Estimate From Work Room _____

Yardage _____   Price _____

Does Price Include Pick Up & Delivery _____

Other Information _____

_____

_____

_____

_____

_____

Form No. 25 (To obtain forms, see page 4.)

upon the information developed by both manufacturers, a checklist for upholstery would have to be so detailed and voluminous as to be unworkable. The recommended procedure on the development of original custom furniture or changes in standard models is to make sketches and confer with the manufacturers.

G. SALES INVOICES
Billing to clients must be handled in a fashion that will clearly indicate the facts to the client, but equally important are control for bookkeeping and reference purposes. Prenumbered invoices should be used and such invoices should be prepared in numerical sequence in triplicate:

1. White copy for the client.

2. Yellow copy for bookkeeping purposes.

3. Pink copy for client's folder.

H. CUSTOMER CREDIT FORMS
Occasionally it becomes necessary to issue a credit to a client for something previously billed. A well-coordinated system calls for credit to be designated to avoid confusion with invoices. Since credits are not issued frequently, they need not be prenumbered, but a numerical sequence should be maintained. The credit numbers can be inserted manually.

The credits should be prepared in triplicate:

1. Pink copy to the client.

2. Blue copy for bookkeeping purposes.

3. Yellow copy for the client's folder.

I. STATEMENTS
Once a month or more frequently, if necessary, the client should be sent a statement indicating the balance due. The statement should reflect the charges to the client and money received or credits given during the specific billing period. The statement need only be prepared in duplicate:

1. White copy for the client.

2. Pink copy for the bookkeeping department or the client's folder.

The preceding samples of invoices, credits, and statements are included to give the designer a basic format to follow. Variations in typography and layout can be made to conform with the designer's own taste in stationery.

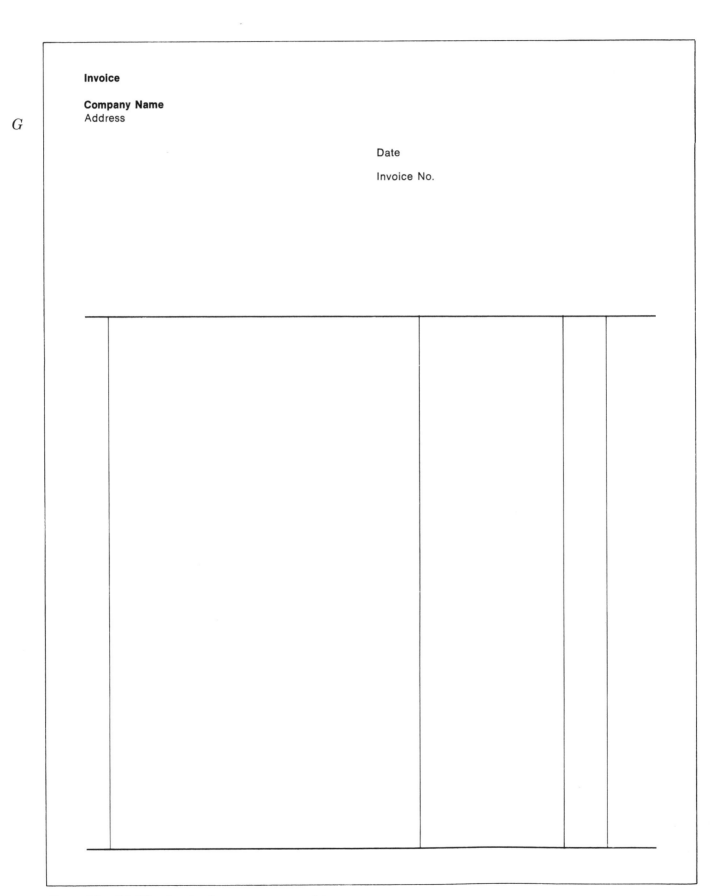

Form No. 26 (To obtain forms, see page 4.)

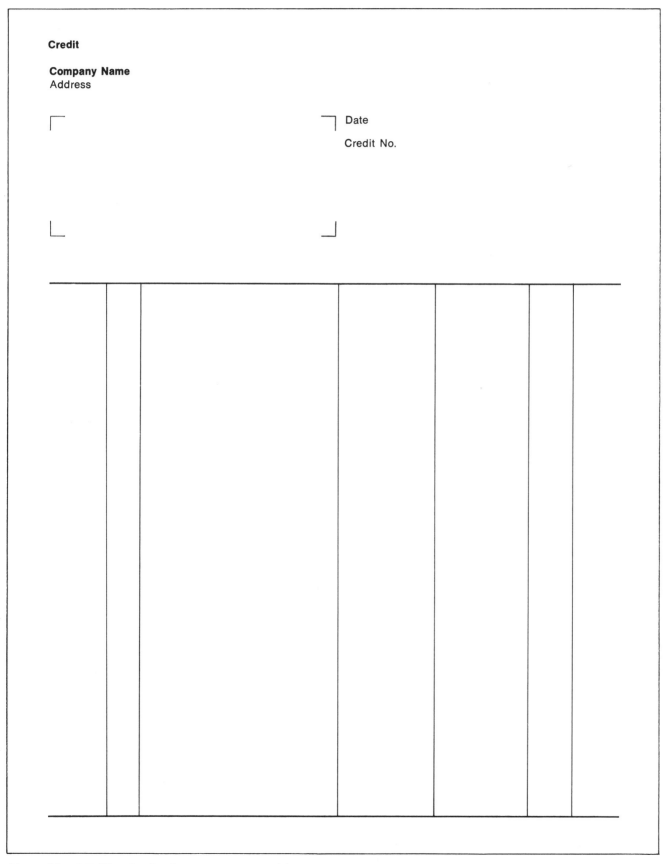

Credit

Company Name
Address

H

Date

Credit No.

Form No. 27 (To obtain forms, see page 4.)

I

Statement

Company Name
Address

Date		Charges	Credit	Balance	

Form No. 28 (To obtain forms, see page 4.)

CHAPTER 31

Basic Elements of Bookkeeping and Accounting for Interior Designers

It has been our experience that interior designers make the worst possible candidates for the bookkeeping profession and certainly bookkeepers would probably make the worst kind of interior designer. However, certain records must be kept—not only for the proper flow of internal procedures and information, but also, and equally important, because various taxing and other governmental agencies require detailed and correct information. Therefore, the interior designer must be aware of the absolute need for proper accounting records.

Accounting records and systems are generally developed, installed, and maintained for functional efficiency by trained accountants. However, the amount of systematizing and degree of complexity of the records depends upon:

1. The size of the organization.

2. The volume of work to be recorded.

3. The necessity to maintain absolutely correct time and cost records for fee and billing purposes.

4. The firm's financial ability to pay for the time of trained staff personnel and outside accountants retained to supervise the work.

THE LARGER ORGANIZATIONS

The interior designer who is the principal or chief executive of a large design firm needs and can afford the services of either:

1. His own professional comptroller who is an employee for the firm and whose responsibility it is to handle all fiscal matters, install proper bookkeeping and accounting systems, and supervise all recordkeeping.

2. An independent certified public accountant who is retained on a fee basis to work with the comptroller or, when there is no comptroller, to complete the installation of the system, supervise the activities of the bookkeeping department, analyze and interpret the financial results of the operation, and generally advise on fiscal and tax matters.

In the interior design field, the accounting system need never be complex or unwieldy. A regular set of books should be maintained (with certain variations and ramifications depending upon the information required).

PRINCIPAL RECORDS

1. Cash receipts journal

2. Cash disbursements journal

3. Sales register

4. Purchase journal or voucher register

5. Petty cash journal

6. Accounts receivable ledger

7. Accounts payable ledger

8. General ledger

9. General journal

The use of these journals is fairly standardized in the business world, and the only comment necessary concerns the sales register and the purchase journal.

The sales register should record and analyze each sales invoice prepared, indicating information sufficient for sales tax purposes and division of income. Exhibit A is a basic format and can be further developed with additional columns, indicating, for example, a further breakdown of the application of sales tax (or nonsales tax) information (depending upon the geographical taxing locality and the omission of sales tax from sales of particular services).

If the designer sells his or her own inventory, a column can be set up in the sales register that indicates such sales and accumulates the necessary information so that the percentage of income as profit from the sale can be compared with the other kinds of income realized by the sale. It is almost axiomatic that while in many other businesses a complete sales register need not be maintained, in the interior design field it is a must because of the very important control information it yields.

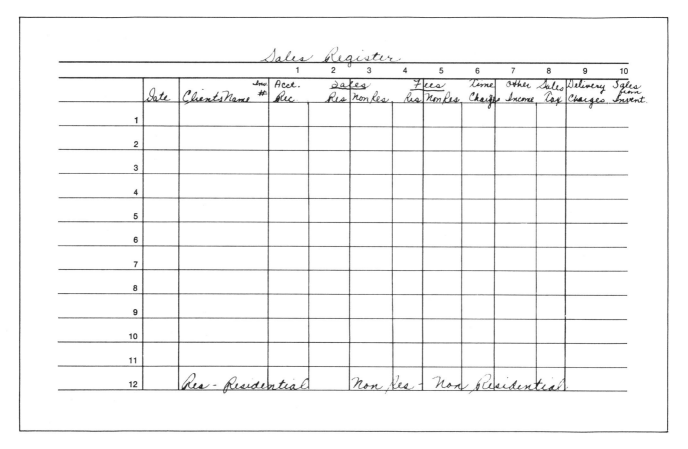

Exhibit B, the purchase journal, is the other register that needs to be detailed here. It should record, in addition to the purchase information, the auxiliary information documented in the sales register, which cross references the client's name to the purchase made:

1. Purchases for residential clients.

2. Purchases for nonresidential clients.

3. Job costs. These columns accumulate cost information that may or may not be billable to the client but that affect the gross profit of each job.

This chapter cannot possibly include a complete set of records or chart of accounts as a standard guide for the profession. A set of standard account books and charts of account breakdowns would be inappropriate for the larger firm, since the detailed records kept and the depth of systematic analysis based upon them depends completely upon the size, functions, and needs of each particular firm. Variations from what accountants would consider standard account books could be set up only by trained accountants or management consultants with a knowledge of the interior design field—or simply through trial-and-error experience. However, our experience indicates that with proper records a design firm can obtain such information about its own operation as shown in the analysis of income sources on page 181, indicating sources of income and direct costs of design. This type of analysis, when carried out and correlated with other expense factors involved in each segment of the income source (derived by comparing the cost of time with the income earned at that same time), can give management an excellent guide to the profitable operation of the business.

WORK IN PROCESS INVENTORY

An important factor involved in proper accounting techniques is the financial effect of work or jobs in process at the time any particular statement is drawn up. *Work in process* is best described as those items of furnishing or services for which a designer has been billed by a trade source and which he or she has not yet billed to the client. To overlook this factor is to arrive at incorrect statement figures.

If the accounting system is set up properly, the work in process is arrived at quite simply. A perfect example is in the client's inventory sheet described in Chapter 16. By referring to that chapter, you will see that the receipt of the source's invoice is noted on the form by a red check mark where the item is listed. Until the item is billed to the client, it is an open item of inventory.*

THE SMALL OR ONE-PERSON FIRM

The interior designer whose firm is a small or one-person type of operation will very often find that he is unable to afford not only a comptroller but a full-time bookkeeper, and even if he can afford a qualified bookkeeper, he hasn't enough work to justify hiring one. He or she can get by adequately with a parttime bookkeeper and/or a periodic visit from an accountant. However, it is necessary for him to devote some of his precious time to maintaining a simple set of basic records so that:

1. Enough information will be readily available at all times, in simple form, to guide and control such everyday financial activities as his or her transactions with clients and trade sources.

2. Information will be easily available in concise and usable form for either a parttime bookkeeper or an accountant, who may come in periodically and/or at the end of the year to pick up the information he or she needs.

3. There will be a base from which to construct tax information and enough financial information so that the designer will be able to interpret and analyze at least some of his or her activities.

By giving a little time to recordkeeping and by

---

*Note: This is true only if the vendor's invoice has been paid or entered in the accounts payable control (if one is maintained).

B

Purchase Journal

		1	2	3	4	5	6	7	8	9	10
		Acct. Payable	Client Purchase Res. Non Res. Inv.			Job Costs Client Charge Non Charge				Other Purchases	
	Date	Vendor										
1												
2												
3												
4												
5												
6												
7												
8												
9												
10												
11												
12												

Analysis of Income Sources

Commercial Fees				
Royalties			600	
Commissions			7200	
Contract Services			10800	
Time charges			4300	
Total Commercial Fees				22900
Residential Fees				
Commissions			13700	
Contract Services			15900	
Time			20100	
Total Residential Fees				49700
Decorating				
Sales - Commercial		16600		
Sales - Residential		362000		
			378600	
Cost of Sales				
Inventory - beginning		63000		
Purchases - Commercial		10600		
Purchases - Residential		230000		
Purchases - Stock		3200		
Freight and Delivery		500		
		307300		
Less: Inventory at End		19000		
Cost of Sales			288300	
Decorating Income				90300

being orderly and neat, the designer can actually reduce expenses and, more important, know what he or she is doing at all times. Without some semblance of order, the mass of papers that must be handled is enough to create limitless confusion. The small design firm must maintain:

1. Records to control the flow of the work in progress.

2. A record of funds received and funds disbursed.

3. A record to control sales and record the sales taxes due to the taxing authorities.

4. A record of financial transactions with trade sources.

5. A record of the clients' financial transactions.

The following exhibits and illustrations will indicate that it is relatively simple and easy to maintain records without being a trained bookkeeper.*

1. Design Work-Flow Records
   The records for controlling work flow have been thoroughly discussed in preceding chapters, and from the material presented, the designer should be able to develop a system with which he or she can work easily.
2. Funds Received and Funds Disbursed
   a. Cash Receipts, Exhibit C
      All moneys received by the designer from every source and deposited in his or her checking account must be listed in a cash receipts book and entered in the appropriate column.
   b. Cash Disbursements, Exhibit D
      A record of every check issued by the designer is made here and entered in the appropriate column.

---

*All amounts used throughout this section are for illustrative purposes only and do not suggest actual costs and expenses.

3. Record of Sales and Sales Taxes, Exhibit E
   Every invoice prepared by the designer to be issued to his or her client is entered in numerical sequence and analyzed in the appropriate columns.
4. Control of Transactions with Trade Sources, Exhibit F
   One of the most annoying problems that the small design firm must face is that of controlling payments to sources and suppliers. Errors can be made in payments, invoices may be paid twice, credit for deposits paid may not be applied to the final account, and so on. The use of purchase control is an effective method of trying to avoid such problems.
5. Transactions with Clients, Exhibit G
   The designer should always maintain a separate account for each client, indicating the moneys received and the invoices issued. Maintaining this ledger account will always indicate quickly what balance a client owes.

In order to understand the use of the recorded memoranda shown in the various exhibits in this chapter, as well as the information derived from them, examples of transactions are provided here and posted to the exhibits.

1. March 1. Designer C. J. Jones deposits $5,000 as initial working capital (entered in Cash Receipts Journal, Exhibit C, line 1).
2. March 4. Pays for stationery by check $120 (entered in Cash Disbursements, Exhibit D, line 1). Pays attorney's fee of $400 (Exhibit D, line 2).
3. March 5. Signs contract with new client Elaine Brown and receives $500 retainer.
   (a. Enter in Cash Receipts Journal, Exhibit C.
   b. Open ledger account for client Elaine Brown in Transactions with Clients, Exhibit G, and enter receipt of money from her.)
4. March 15. Client Elaine Brown signs a confirmation to purchase the following items

C

	Date	Received From	Amount (1)	(2)	Balance Due from Client (3)	(4)	Deposit from Client (5)	(6)	(7)	(8)	Other Item (9)	Amount (10)
Cash Receipts									Month of _____ 19 ___			
1	Mar 1	C. J. Jones	5000 –								Capital	5000
2	Mar 5	Elaine Brown	500 –					500 –				
3	Mar 15	Elaine Brown	1220					1220 –				
4	Mar 25	Elaine Brown	210 –		210 –							
5												
6												
7			6930 –		210 –		1720 –					5000 –
8												
9												
10												
11												
12												

D

Cash Disbursements   Month of _____ 19__

	Date	To Whom Paid	Check #	1 Amount	2	3 Purchases For client	4	5 amount	6 Stock	7 Personal Drawing	8 Petty Cash	9 other Item	10 amt
1	Mar 4	A&C Stationers	101	120—								Stationery	120.00
2	4	Frank Smith	102	400—								Legal	400—
3	15	Alan Furn. Co.	103	630—		Brown–Deposit		630—					
4	15	Gerald Fab. Co.	104	110—		^	^	110—					
5	21	John Jones	105	150—						100—	50—		
6	21	Carol Antique Shop	106	300—					300				
7	26	Gerald Fab. Co	107	110—		Brown Balance		110—					
8													
9				1820				850—	300—	100—	50—		520
10													
11													
12													

E

Sales   Month of ——— 19——

		Name	Inv #	1 amount	2	3 Sales Txble	4 Non Txble	5 Sales Tax	6 Freight	7 Fees	8	9 Other Item	10 Amt.
1	Mar 22	Elaine Brown	101	380.00		340–		17–	23–				
2	26	Elaine Brown	102	2300–		2100–		105–	95–				
3													
4				2680–		2440–		122–	118–				
5													
6													
7													
8													
9													
10													
11													
12													

F

			1	2	3	4	5	6	7	8	9	10
			Amount of Invoice	Paid Date	Check #		Deposits with Date	Amt	Vendor offset	Billed to Client Date	Inv #	Amt.
1	Mar 15	Alan Furniture Co					3/15	630–				
2	15	Gerald Fabrics Co					3/15	110–	3/26(c)			
3	21	Gerald Fabrics Co	220–	3/26	#107(a)					3/22	101	340–
4	26	Alan Furniture Co	1260–		(B)					3/26	102	2100–
5	27	Vita Trucking Co	95–							3/26	102	95–
6										note C		

Vendor's Control   Month of   19__

7 Note (a) Deposit of $110 to Gerald Fabrics Co. is coupled with payment for the balance
8   to indicate that the vendors invoice is fully paid.
9 Note (b) Alan Furniture Co invoice of $1260 is open and unpaid but there is a
10   deposit of $630 which has not been offset leaving a balance of $630 –
11 Note (c) This record of Vendor's Control can be used as a control
12   for billing purposes.

G

Sheet No.					Account No.				
Terms					Name *Client Account – Elaine Brown*				
Rating					Address				
Credit Limit									
Date 19........	Items Charged to Client	Folio	√	Debits	Date 19........	Items Received from Client	Folio	√	Credits
Mar. 22	Inv. #101		a	380.00	Mar 5	Retainer – apply to Final Bal.			500 –
26	Inv. #102			2300.00	15	Confirmation Deposit $1220			
						Sofa & Chair			1050 –
						Fabric		a	170 –
					25	Payment		a	210 –

Note (a) Since the client paid the invoice for the fabric first
with a deposit of 170.00 and then a payment for the balance
the transaction is complete and the items are lettered off (a) to
indicate no balance for that particular invoice.

The next time completely paid will be lettered off (b), the next (c) and
so on.

and gives the designer a 50 percent deposit of $1,220.

Sofa	$1,500
Club chair	600
17 yards of fabric	340
	$2,440

(Enter receipt of cash in ledger account for Elaine Brown in Cash Receipts, Exhibit C.)

5. March 15. Designer places the orders for this merchandise and is required to give deposits to the vendors. Designer writes the following checks:

| Alan Furniture Co. | $630 |
| Gerald Fabric Co. | $110 |

(Enter in Cash Disbursements, Exhibit D, and in Control of Transactions with Trade Sources, Exhibit F.)

6. March 21. Designer draws check for $150, $100 for personal use and $50 for reimbursement of petty cash expenses. (Enter in Cash Disbursements, Exhibit D.)
7. March 21. Designer buys an antique lamp for $300 from Carol Antiques for inventory. (Enter in Exhibit D.)
8. March 21. Receives invoice from Gerald Fabric Co. due March 28 for $220. (Enter in first column only of Control of Transactions with Trade Sources, Exhibit F.)
9. March 22. Makes out invoice #101 for client Elaine Brown for fabric:

Fabric	$340
Sales tax 5%	$ 17
Delivery charge	$ 23
Total	$380
Less paid on A/C (Confirmation #1)	$170
Balance due	$210

(Enter in the Sales Journal, in the Record of Sales and Sales Taxes, Exhibit E, and client's account in Transactions with Clients, Exhibit G).

10. March 25. Client Elaine Brown pays invoice #101 for fabric for $210. (Enter in Cash Receipts, Exhibit C, and in Elaine Brown's ledger sheet in Transactions with Clients, Exhibit G.)
11. March 26. Designer pays Gerald Fabric Co. balance due of $110. (Enter in Cash Disbursements, Exhibit D, and in Control of Transactions with Trade Sources, Exhibit F, indicating date of payment.)
12. March 26. Receives invoice from Alan Furniture Co. for sofa and chair for $1,260. (Enter in Exhibit F.)
13. March 26. Client Elaine Brown billed with invoice #102:

Sofa	$1,500
Chair	600
	$2,100
5% sales tax	105
	$2,205
Freight	95
	$2,300
Less deposit	1,050
	$1,250

(Enter in Sales Journal in Record of Sales and Sales Taxes, Exhibit E, and client's account in Transactions with Clients, Exhibit G.)

14. March 27. Receives invoice from Vita Trucking Co. for freight charges of $95. (Enter in Control of Transactions with Trade Sources, Exhibit F.)

At this point if you review the entries made in the books, you will find:

Exhibit C: Deposited	$6,930
From the following sources:	
Investment	$5,000
Received from client	$1,930
Exhibit D: Disbursed for month	$1,820
Payments for client's goods	$ 850

Purchased inventory	$ 300
Personal use	$ 100
Petty cash	$ 50
Stationery	$ 120
Legal	$ 400

Exhibit E: Sales for the month	$2,680
Of which taxable sales are	$2,440
Due for sales taxes	$ 122
Reimbursement for delivery and freight charges	$ 118

Exhibit F: Indicates balance due to	
Alan Furniture Co.	$ 630
Invoice $1,260 less open deposit of	$ 630
Invoice due to Vita Trucking Co.	$ 95

This exhibit also indicates that all goods and services purchased for clients have been billed out. (This is another method of inventory control.)

Exhibit G: Client Account for Elaine Brown

Invoice #101 has been paid in full.

Invoice #102 for $2,300 is unpaid, except there is a deposit of $1,050, leaving a balance of $1,250 to be collected. In addition the designer has a $500 retainer that can be applied against the account at any time.

THE DAILY DIARY

The designer's daily diary is another simple recording device that plays an important and necessary role in accumulating information. It should be used to accomplish the following two purposes:

1. To record time, not only to give the designer feedback on the allocation of his or her time, but to record time spent with a client.

2. To record out-of-pocket business expenses for which the designer should be reimbursed, since they are valid deductions for tax purposes. At the present time the tax department requires that a record of expenses be maintained, indicating *when, where, why*, and *with whom* the expenditure is made. The diary is now accepted as a record by the Internal Revenue Service if maintained properly.

The diary should be recorded in the following manner:

Monday, March 4
11:00 A.M. to client Elaine Brown's, taxi $4.60.
3:00 P.M. return to office, taxi $4.80.

Tuesday, March 5
With client Elaine Brown at Gerald Fabric Co. showroom, 11:00 to 11:45 A.M. Lunch with Elaine Brown at Pablo's, $18.80. With client Elaine Brown at Alan Furniture showroom, 1:30 to 2:30 P.M.
Taxis from Pablo's to showrooms and return to office, $7.60.

If the diary is maintained as indicated, the designer can cull information from it to record on time accumulation forms. He or she is also able to reconstruct expenses for reimbursement and to show a permanent backup record for tax purposes.

Index